COVER ME IN GOLD: THE HISTORY, HORRORS & OTHER UNKNOWN FACTS ABOUT GOLD

DAWDU M. AMANTANAH

U.E Publishing

CONTENTS

Manufactured in the United States of America

Cover Me in Gold/ Mahama. Amantanah. —1st edition © 2019

ISBN 978-0-578-72528-4

LITERATURE ALSO BY DAWDU M. AMANTANAH

Death of a Rose Rise of the Black Petunia

The Bit on Digital Coins: A Quick Practical Guide to Understanding Cryptocurrency

QUOTE

Gold is worshipped in all climates, without a single temple, and by all classes, without a single hypocrite.

-Charles Caleb Colton

ACKNOWLEDGMENTS

First and foremost, thank you, God, for giving me the ability to write with passion and perseverance. Aunty Donna, I express my sincere gratitude to you for giving me the knowledge of the importance of education and the love for reading at a young age despite the adversity of having it better than some and worse than others. Granny, thank you. Thank you, dad rest well. Thank you, mom. Thank you, Satin, no need to add your last name because it will be the same as mine soon. You are my number one confidant when it comes to any of my books I write and any crazy ideas I come up with.

I want to thank Benjamin Wade, my illustrator for this book; you're the closest entity I've met to Picasso and a dear friend, for seeing my vision. Matthias, without you, this book wouldn't have reached readers until a much later date. Thanks for your generosity in removing a major roadblock in getting this project to completion. Salute. Junia Yearwood, thank you for your editing ability and years of experience teaching the art of English; your proofreading is top-notch and has not gone unnoticed.

This book, *Cover Me in Gold*, required a lot of research material, and I am grateful to the Central Library for allowing me access to so much knowledge on gold. Shout out to Olive Tree Books N Voices for always supporting my literary work. Thank you to all the interesting people and tour guides I met while traveling abroad in search of gold's unique subculture. Finally, to all the people I may have forgotten that continue to have an interest in gold, silver and the history of all things shiny, thank you for picking up this book as your form of an enjoyable read.

INTRODUCTION

One of the most beautiful metals of the natural world, gold has been a standard fixture in the history of humans for over six thousand years due to the scarcity, mysticism, and wealth it generates. The stories ahead tell of gold's intoxicating effects on humanity; it is a substance like no other, and the value of it has awakened the evil of greed in both men and women. For much of human history, the motive behind war, conquest, wealth, and world exploration has been the desperation to acquire gold.

Gold's beginnings from simple adornment to being the bedrock of monetary systems and investment shows this element cannot be created by humans in large enough quantities to offset the enormous financial cost of the machinery and technology it demands. I wrote *Cover Me in Gold* to give the reader insight into these stories, topics, and much more.

In this book, I give a snapshot of the history, people, events, and myths that surround gold and silver that I found interesting, but the information is not in any particular historical order. All the information in this book can be found with tentative research. It's no secret; it is public knowledge, but like mining for gold, it takes a lot of work. I genuinely feel if you read this book with an open mind, it will change the way you look at the history of precious metals.

I've always been obsessed with gold. I'm not sure if it's due to its shiny nature, my astrological ascendant, or the past years I've spent working in the finance industry. I was curious about what they never told us about gold in history class, so I researched it. My method of getting gold's impact straight was through exploring historical and contemporary information on gold and silver to the best of my ability with the hope it can become a teaching tool for me and others in the future.

This is my perspective on gold and silver through tireless research from experts on the topic, which include articles, books, visiting the US Mint, and my travels to ancient Mayan sites like Chichén Itzá in Mexico. Traveling to some of these places allowed me to fully engulf myself in gold's impact on history and economics. However, the information in this book is sold with the understanding that the author is not engaged in any rendering of financial, spiritual, or professional advice, especially disclaiming any liability that is incurred if you chose to invest in or study precious metals. Research of gold's origins and uses have intrigued astrophysicists, alchemists, and the wealthy for centuries due to gold being virtually indestructible.

Humans age, then die; as gold ages, it becomes more timeless and valuable. The narratives that arise from gold have filled history books, and the minds of people looking to enrich their lives. The pages of this book are filled with similar information. Gold's appeal is universal, yet the historical impact, investment potential, esoteric value, and medical aspects of this precious metal are rarely discussed in depth. Gold is a metal that is truly alien, only made in explosive collisions far away in the galaxy.

According to new scientific research, gold is abundant on other planets such as Mercury and Mars. Supernova explosions in space eject precious metallic particles throughout the cosmos, which become embedded in the soil of various planets in the solar system,

Earth being one of them. Obviously, mining gold in space would be a real challenge at our current stage of exploration, but once we deem it possible and profitable to mine space gold, its value would be considerable. On Earth, gold can be found everywhere financial dependability is demanded, and it does not show much promise of slowing down.

The same gold under our feet created the gold rush, the Bretton Woods system, and even remedies to cure the body of ailments. Gold comprises one gram per every thousand tons of soil with those odds that would give someone roughly the same odds of finding a grain of sand in a swimming pool as they would a grain of gold dust, but there is much more to gold than its yellow shine and bright luster. Gold is held in the highest regard when introduced in religion. Valued well before the birth of Jesus Christ, gold will remain coveted as a substance and a medium of exchange that has modified human history and culture.

Almost every culture on Earth understands gold represents wealth, timelessness, and regality; silver has been used in jewelry, coins, and as a tonic for thousands of years. Pharaohs were buried with gold in the ancient past with the understanding their wealth could be used in the afterlife, as gold was thought to be the supernatural flesh of the sun god Amun Ra. Lavishing themselves with it ensured immortality. In Buddhism, gold represents good health and happiness, so finding Buddha depicted in gold is extremely common. During Buddhist ceremonies, monks would pray in temples at the feet of pure gold Buddha statues in search of enlightenment and purity, with some weighing up to five tons like the Golden Buddha of Wat Traimit. After receiving the proper financing from Spain's King Ferdinand and Queen Isabella, gold has driven men like the Italian explorer Christopher Columbus to conquer unforgiving oceans to a new world, leaving discovery and colonization in his wake[1]

This incorruptible metal may be the closest thing to God in many aspects. In the book of Exodus from the Old Testament, Moses relays the instructions from the Lord: "Tell the Israelites to bring me an offering. You are to receive the offering for me from everyone whose heart prompts them to give. These are the offerings you are to receive from them: gold, silver, and bronze." Once Moses reached Mount Sinai, he began to receive offerings for the holy tabernacle that was to be built to house the ten commandments in gold. Gold was a common topic in religions all across the world, with some embracing it and others shunning it.

Not all people believe in gold's mysticism and consider it a useless metal, not because it's not worth anything. Mainly to the fact that most gold is not used at all, just stored away in vaults except in cases of personal adornment or barter. As we use more technology, more gold is required due to it being a good conductor. Approximately twelve percent of the world's gold stocks are used in electronics and other related industries. Gold is edible and flavorless. It has been used in cuisine as an additive for centuries.

Olympians compete for gold medals, and some musicians aspire to achieve gold-selling albums. Humans are so gold crazy it is held on the pedestal of achievement all around us. Whether worn as a status symbol around the necks of budding hip-hop artists expressing veneration for their record labels or stacked in bars of bullion in Fort Knox's vaults, gold's mysticism has found its way into every aspect of our society. There should be no surprise empires have risen and fallen with the ebb and flow of shiny metals because there is just something magical about gold and silver.

Like an onion, gold allegedly has many layers of history, taboos, and healing secrets. If you are open to wisdom, gold may help you to receive that wisdom easier. Gold is said to be good for people with insecurities or self-esteem issues. It builds confidence, balances your mood, and allows people who wear it to feel more in control. Whether that is true or not, most people you see wearing a lot of gold usually have a smile on their faces, radiant skin, and an air of great importance.

The final premise of *Cover Me in Gold* is to give people a great form of storytelling that is not only informative but also fun, full of factoids, mysterious stories, and history of what precious metals are and how gold's arcane culture intoxicated man in the past, present, and future. Any and everyone can dig into this book and find something that interests them or makes them fall in love with gold all over again.

1

GOLD'S ORIGINS FORGED IN THE COSMOS

Since humans have lived on this planet, gold has been treasured as the divine and noble metal. The first questions you may ask about gold are easy. Where does it come from? How was it created? Truly, a direct answer to the question, it would take years of study and research into gold's origins.

Astronomers who have conducted tedious research have concluded that gold is a mineral element heated and forged over three billion years ago as the metallic by-product of exploding stars. Marina Koren, a staff writer for *The Atlantic,* explains how science is uncovering the secrets to the cosmic collisions that created plumes of heavy metals filled with gold. "Astronomers studied the spectra—the chemical composition of cosmic objects—of the collision and found that the plume ejected by the merger contained a host of newly formed heavy chemical elements, including gold, silver, platinum, and others."

These mergers create cosmic objects on a grand scale throughout the vast universe. Throwing out a number like a million or 500 million would be an understatement of the exact amount it contains. Gold and stars have a deep connection solely because gold can be created only from them, nothing else.[1] Some stars wander the cosmos like ships in a vast ocean; other stars move in clusters like stacked pool balls. During their journey over millions of years and great distances, stars occasionally collide with one another. The merger of two neutron stars hitting in space creates something explosive, magical, and rare. Through these collisions, or when a supernova—the scientific name for a neutron star—implodes, the stars run out of fuel. This causes a star's gravity to collapses into itself, choking off heat, energy, and light. These explosions can be so massive throughout the cosmos that they are only a few notches less extreme than a gamma-ray explosion. The creation of precious metals has a connection to stars with explosive evidence, similar to how the rocky makeup of our world was formed. A star, like a human, is born, lives in the cosmos, then dies. How it affects the universe after it dies depends on the mass of the star. A star with low mass creates a white dwarf; a star with high mass creates a black hole, and a star with average mass becomes a neutron star.

A neutron star is made up mostly of the element hydrogen and a multitude of protons and electrons bouncing around in the star's core. This superheated mass of extreme gravitational pressure, coupled with hydrogen molecules colliding and squeezing together, builds a superheated reaction called "nuclear fusion." Nuclear fusion creates the same powerful combustion it would take to make a hydrogen bomb. Trillions of hydrogen atoms fire off intense energy to produce heat, and this heat is what gives the star its bright glow and extreme temperature.

This display of blaze and glory, however, does not last forever. As the star ages, the hydrogen molecules give off other by-product elements such as helium and carbon, causing neutrons to emerge and preparing the mass of flaming gas for its next phase in the star's life cycle. The continual buildup of these elements become heavy, increasing the star's size and changing its color. Iron and nickel begin to form from the buildup, and this elemental reaction repeats until nuclear fusion runs out, choking the star of its last bit of fuel. The lack of fuel creates inward pressure and gravitational shock waves, causing the star's atmosphere to collapse and explode. During this explosion, tiny heated particles of precious metal are shot throughout the universe. The energy from this outward mass of debris can be seen billions of light-years away. These particles of stardust and debris become the building blocks that create heavy metals like silver, uranium, platinum, and gold. Once the stardust collects in large quantities in space and within other celestial bodies, it forms silt and collects in large rocks that become locked in the gravitational orbit of newly created stars.[2]

Over thousands of years, the frigid cold of interstellar space gradually cools the bits of stardust, ice, and rock enough to develop a crusty layer of the mantle. The heavier elements like gold, silver, and platinum sink deeper into the interior of the mantle, and lighter elements naturally rose closer to the surface. All the gold within Earth's crust contains ancient bits of a star that died a very long time ago. Gold also arrived on Earth from meteorite impacts, which were a regular occurrence during Earth's early development.

These meteorites contained large deposits of metallic elements that upon impact lodged and collected into Earth's crust. Liquefied gold was pushed to the surface through geothermic eruptions, settling within Earth's multiple layers of rocky sediment in tiny cracks and veins. Surprisingly, most of the gold on Earth is spread out in small concentrations in seawater, plants, rocks, and even animals.The truth is, gold is everywhere; it's just hard to get in quantities worth people's time and effort, as reporter Angela Chen for *The Verge* explains: "Gold is present in nature, and, on average, the concentration of gold is about 0.5 grams of gold for every one ton of material. So, if you go into your garden and start digging after you make a big hole and dig out one ton of soil material, you have the chance to find half a gram of gold. That's the average concentration on Earth. Of course, in some places, gold is more concentrated, like gold mines or gold bearing quartz veins. In places that are gold abundant, you dig one ton of material, and you could possibly find five or six grams of gold."

Human beings are not exempt from gold's reach, although not in large amounts. Every person has little milligrams of gold flowing through his or her red blood cells and body fluids, but let's explain the dynamics of what makes it precious. The term *precious* could have developed due to gold having intense energy associated with the Sun and silver having a strong association with the Moon. The many ancient cultures that worshipped the Sun did so for a good reason. As studies revealed thousands of years later, gold's origins link to the stars in its earliest moments, meaning these people who existed thousands of years ago were spot on.

People who worshipped celestial objects in the sky, like the ancient civilization of the Inca, called the precious metal gold "*Sweat of the Sun*" due to its yellow brightness, an embodiment of warmth, and sun-like power. The Romans were the first to use hydraulic mining and considered gold the muscle of war as it funded their campaigns to colonize Eastern Europe and North Africa. Once you research and think about how fantastic gold is and how these civilizations understood metallic elements well enough to revere and exploit precious metals as extraordinary, mysterious, and lucrative, it is mind-blowing. Although gold is malleable (easily workable) and ductile (not brittle), the structure of gold is unique because it is highly resistant to harsh chemicals and most acids, with a high atomic weight and massive specific gravity. A tiny piece of gold can be drawn, stretched, or hammered into lightweight sheets or thin wire. Due to its softness, pure, twenty-four-karat gold has the texture of putty.

Over time, exposure to the elements can turn the color of most metals, like copper, green, and iron into rust, but not gold. Gold is timeless and inert; it fails to tarnish or change chemically over time. If you look up the reactivity series chart, you will find interesting results. "Gold is near the bottom of the chart because it is almost unreactive. Only a mixture of concentrated nitric acid and hydrochloric acid (called "*aqua regia*") would dissolve gold"[3] Even when dissolved by the corrosive acid aqua regia, gold is not lost, only liquefied, and can be extracted back to its solid form and accurate weight. Gold is a pure element that has an atomic number of seventy-nine, meaning for every one gold atom, seventy-nine protons reside fixed in its nucleus.

Gold is one of two pure colored metals in existence that requires no additional additives. The other is copper. Gold's massive gravity has an atomic weight of one hundred and ninety-seven with no compounds of other substances mixed into its purest form. Let's gain a better understanding of what massive specific gravity means; here is an example. A small amount of gold can be very dense and heavy for its size. Thanks to gravity, gold may look small until you pick it up and realize how looks can be deceiving, but that's not the only trick gold has up its sleeve.

Many people enjoy hiking in the mountains and lodging in high altitudes as a contributor to their health and vigor. Little do they know mountains are full of gold vein deposits and that gold is radiated off the mountain and the surrounded areas giving the area a natural healing quality. Most of the gold is in the Earth's core, residing 1,800 miles below our feet. The Earth's core contains enough gold to cover the surface seventeen inches thick.

The world's largest gold bar, at the Toi Gold Museum in Japan, measures 17.9 in × 8.9 in × 6.7 in, which is not that big by measurement standards, but it weighs 551 pounds. For a bar of gold that could fit a box, that's pretty heavy. Gold melts and can be shaped at 1,063 degrees Celsius, making it possible to smelt over a fire, making it one of the most easily worked metals in history. Gold and silver are the cosmos gifts to mankind, and new discoveries for its usage are just untapped.

INTERESTING FACTS YOU MAY NOT KNOW ABOUT GOLD & SILVER

Gold

- Soft yellow metal
- Has no taste
- Has no smell
- Will not react with acids
- Good conductor of heat
- Melts at 1,063 degrees Celsius
- Does not tarnish when exposed to oxygen
- Soft and easily worked into thin sheets, thin wire or jewelry
- Gold has been discovered on every continent on earth.
- Gold is edible. Some Native American tribes believed consuming gold could allow humans to levitate.
- Our bodies contain about 0.2 milligrams of gold, most of it in our blood.
- Olympic Gold Medals only contain 1.34% of gold.
- Gold has many uses aside from its monetary and symbolic value. Among other applications, it is used in electronics, electrical wiring, dentistry, electronics, medicine, radiation shielding, and to color glass.

- The world's oceans contain nearly 20 million tons of gold.
- Indian housewives hold 11% of the World's Gold. That is more than the reserves of the U.S., IMF, Switzerland and Germany put together.
- Injecting gold into the body can help fight cancer.
- Apple recovered 2,204 pounds of gold from broken iPhones in 2015. That's worth about US$40 million.

Silver

- A soft, white metal
- Forms alloys with copper to give it additional strength
- Scarce metal
- Best natural reflector of light
- Melts at 960 Celsius
- Tarnishes when exposed to polluted air
- Best conductor of electricity of any metal
- Best conductor of heat of any metal
- Antibacterial and Antiviral
- Can be fashioned into a type of colloidal tonic for drinking but must be used with caution
- Helps with detox
- Eases child birth
- Thwarts negative energy
- Improves speech
- Represents the Moon

Chinese Emperors, Aristocrats, and Empresses used silver chopsticks for over 2,500 years throughout many dynasties. The silver was believed to tarnish when in contact with poison in food—revered only for the rich any commoners caught with silver chopsticks sometimes faced execution. Gold coins or gold leaf was` added to white rice to replenish the minerals in the body. Edible gold is still honored in Chinese society and can still be found served at fancy Chinese restaurants.

2

THE SHINING DAWN OF THE ANCIENT WORLD

In antiquity, gold became the shining dawn of the ancient world for its religious devotion, immortality, and aesthetic quality. The word *gold* in Latin is *aurum,* meaning "shining dawn," Since its discovery, the yellow metal has lived up to its name. The indigenous Alkebulan being the oldest known people in the world, were the first to unearth gold and its unique properties. Alkebulan was the ancient name for Africa before the Romans renamed it. In places like ancient Lydia, the discovery of gold at the surface level put the first gold and silver coins into circulation, according to Greek historian Herodotus, often referred to as "the Father of History."

The ancient Egyptians increased their devotion to gold during this time, displaying it in amulets and the decoration of temples, monuments, and sarcophagi. Gold was so revered in the ancient world that attempts to use alchemy to duplicate it from base metals such as lead were the likely forerunner of chemistry. If abused or taken without permission gold has according to myth carry bad luck or even death.

In some circumstances involving other kingdoms, gold and silver were worn by both men and women, for example, in the Sumer civilization. The royal graves of Ur, dating back to 2500 BC, were unearthed to reveal hundreds of graves rich with gold treasures. King

Agamemnon, the Greek army leader, made famous in the Trojan War of Homer's *Iliad,* is etched in time with the gold "death mask of Agamemnon," a beaten gold funeral mask that found at a Mycenaean gravesite thought to be the kings.

The mask predates Agamemnon by 400 years but remains evidence that his kingdom was rich in gold, ivory, and bronze. The discovery of electrum, a silver-rich gold ore, and gold's ability to mix with other metal alloys such as zinc, copper, and silver made it an obsession with adornment for goldsmiths power for the old ruling bureaucracy. Most ancient religions worshipped the Sun, and gold represented the cooled sweat from the solar system's most significant energy source. The quantity of gold mined and hoarded in ancient times is impossible to gauge. Many ancient civilizations like Babylon, Africa, Rome, Persia, and Mesopotamia reveal the beginnings of gold's impactful influence on humankind.[1]

During these ancient golden ages, gold slowly started becoming a form of money and more as a form of worship and spirituality. Gold becomes an important component of humanity's soul potential, whether that meant protection in the afterlife or the current one. Gold allowed man to create individually and collectively on Earth like never before in history. The hoarding and exchanging of gold aided in building empires and kingdoms, and in other dark forms such as funding wars and hostile takeovers.

People of the ancient past were more in tune with consciousness and how certain metallic elements worked in correspondence with the human body that is now being rediscovered. Silver kept the body cool and blood pressure at bay. The shining dawn was held in importance from Tibet to India to the Middle East down towards Africa and Europe. Techniques to add gold and silver in ancient kings' pockets, Queen's and Pharaohs paved the way for some of history's greatest stories and tales of chaos.

DID YOU KNOW?

Author Zecharia Sitchin famous for his books on pseudoscience and pseudohistory theorized that an alien race called "the Anunnaki" came from another planet in our solar system that has a 3,600-year elliptical orbit. The Anunnaki planet was suffering due to a dying ozone layer that forced them to seek a planet with dense gold reserves. The Anunnaki's home planet needed gold in the atmosphere to restore the ozone and came to Earth to mine gold and take it back to their home planet.

QUEEN PUABI & THE ROYAL TREASURE GRAVES OF UR

Situated in the southern desert of Iraq, Ur's ancient city mentioned in the Holy Bible, Torah, and Quran. Although many archeologists are conflicted on the site's exact location, believed to be Abraham's birthplace, a patriarch for the Jewish, Islam, and Christian faiths. Beyond its religious history, thousands of years ago when the ancient Sumer civilization was in its golden dynasty, a mysterious queen buried in a tomb laden with wild treasures of stunning gold, silver, and beautiful gemstones. It was untouched for several millennia.

After its discovery in 1922, Sir Charles Leonard Woodley, a British archaeologist known for his careful record keeping, worked tirelessly for twelve years excavating the ruins of Ur in Mesopotamia for the British Museum. Sir Leonard Woodley found three-cylinder seals among the well-preserved coffins buried in the royal cemetery complex. The Ur royal scripts mentioned Shubad on the seals as the woman given an elaborate burial. She also went by another name. In Sumerian cuneiform, the words composed her name and title as Puabi, sometimes mistakenly read as Nin or Shubad, meaning queen or great lady, but this is somewhat still in dispute. There is no mention of her on the Sumerian king's list, so she predates the first dynasty of Ur.

Woodley discovered thousands of graves during his excavations. Sixteen were considered royal burials for the elite of Mesopotamian society and contained items only the finest goldsmiths of the day could have created. Timothy Green, who wrote *The Ages of Gold,* states "The most spectacular finds in these 'death pits,' were in the graves of King Abargi and Queen Puabi, dating back to 2600 BC." Maintaining its precious allure in this early civilization, gold played a huge role in death. Woodley's team sifted through the royal cemetery's cluttered remains and discovered more and more spectacular finds, including a gold dagger, gold bowls, and a queen's tomb filled with all thing's gold and shiny. There is much more mystery and, in some instances, weird rituals involved with Queen Puabi's tomb besides its huge stash of gold items. Kings and queens who died did so with all the treasures, animals, and attendants that served them in life.

The high preists buried Queen Puabi with dozens of her attendants. The day of burial, two of her most loyal servants were buried in the chamber with her, one crouched at her head, the other at her feet. The most loyal of these servants were suspected of having consumed poison. In contrast, others were poisoned by others or attacked and sacrificed by blunt-force trauma to fulfill a ritual honor by the high priests during burial. Journal article "*Hidden Treasure from the Royal Cemetery at Ur*" details how well adorned the attendants who partook in the sacrifice looked. "The bodies of sixty-eight women were found in the main pit area. The women were laid out in ordered rows running northwest to southeast. All were heavily adorned with gold, silver, lapis lazuli and carnelian jewelry."

Once Charles Woodley found the queen's remains, he was blown away at how preserved the gold artifacts remained. He recorded how Queen Puabi's hands held a golden cup, and her head was decorated with an exquisite headdress. It was an extravagant display of gold leaves, flowers, and rings intertwined in a wig decorated with a lapis lazuli crest and a gold comb to make it look like a bouquet.

Massive crescent-shaped gold earrings long rotted off the body lay dormant in the tomb, still gleaming. A string of semiprecious stones covered her upper body. A bright yellow gold and blue lapis lazuli bracelet, still as beautiful as the day it was made, was wrapped around the queen's wrists. Some of the most outrageous items buried with the queen were exotic animals and a chariot adorned with a lionesses' head made of fine silver. Various stones and pottery vessels also were piled around the walls of the chamber. Sumer pioneered civilization, laying the foundation for royalty's connection to gold in the afterlife for generations to come.

DID YOU KNOW?

Sir Isaac Newton despite his great achievements in the scientific revolution and the laws of motion also had a huge impact on the gold standard. In 1696, he became Warden of the Royal Mint, taking on the great responsibility of recoinage investigating coin clippers and even carrying out his gold and silver assay.

TWO ROMAN'S THAT RECEIVED DEATH BY DRINKING MOLTEN GOLD.

Marcus Lincinius Crassus (115-53 BCE) was the wealthiest general and politician in Roman history. A man emboldened by his achievements in real estate and on the battlefield. His vast wealth and savvy political skills brought him two consulships and influence into the upper echelon of Roman politics. Julius Caesar even sought his counsel and was mentored by Crassus early in his career as an emperor.

Slavery, bribery, scamming, warfare, and even arson sum up just a few of the ways Crassus gained his wealth. "According to Plutarch, Crassus had accumulated the vast sum of 7,100 talents, had extensive real estate interests, owned silver mines, possessed a huge number of slaves, and, of course, he was able to fund his army." Crassus played a considerable part in creating the First Triumvirate (Julius Caesar, Pompey, and Crassus), an uneasy alliance between Rome's three most powerful men. The Triumvirate significantly contributed to his rise to the top of state affairs. Still, his long search for a military triumph to match Pompey's great rival would ultimately bring about his downfall.

During his time spent trying to conquer the Parthian Empire, Crassus extorted vast riches from the local populations in the places he could control. Crassus wintered in Syria for several months, allowing the Parthians to prepare an attack. It didn't take long before Crassus suffered one significant loss after another. The Armenian king Artavasdes II deserted him in battle, and his son, P. Licinius Crassus, was killed in an attack. An army of 10,000 strong led by the Parthian king gave the remaining Roman legions under Crassus's command their last devastating blow. Vastly outnumbered and suffering heat exhaustion from the unfamiliar desert climate, the Roman army crumbled under the Parthian pressure. "Consequently, the Romans were encircled, trapped, and forced to surrender arms and their Eagle standards."

According to legend, while imprisoned, Marcus Crassus attempted to bribe his captures, but the offer was refused. Allegedly, Crassus was sentenced to a gruesome and unusual execution. The Parthian king ordered Crassus to be killed by having molten gold poured down his throat, symbolic of his unquenchable thirst for wealth.

Valerian the Elder (195–260 AD) was a Roman emperor and experienced senator. He came to power at the age of fifty-three in the middle of the third century's Roman crisis. The third century was a dangerous time to be emperor. In fifty years, Rome went through twenty different emperors, none lasting more than a few months in power. During this period, Roman emperors were targeted and assassinated by their rivals, various poisons, and even their troops.

Valerian the Elder seemed to beat the odds of past emperors and ruled for a long seven years with the promise of bringing order to the Roman Empire, which was apparently out of control.

Valerian's predecessors had been ignoring the Persian attacks against the Roman empire in the east. News broke the Goths sacked Athens city, adding to Rome's heel's already accumulating thorns. Valerian marched into Asia minor to quell the goths and arrived in Mesopotamia to aid a fellow general whose army was ravaged by disease and had little moral. After a devastating defeat at the Battle of Edessa, the emperor chose to negotiate a peace treaty with the Persian king.

In 260 A.D, together with his general staff, Valerian met with Shapur to discuss terms, but the meeting turned into a trap. Valerian was imprisoned, tormented, and embarrassed. Shapur made Valerian his slave, which involved living a life of pity as he was dragged in chains and forced to bend down so Shapur could step on the emperor's back to mount his horse.

Due to Valerian's death occurring over a thousand years ago, a few versions of what transpired next. In the first account, Shapur expressed his hatred for Valerian by pouring molten gold down the captured emperor's throat, proving to Rome money could not buy victory in battle. In the second account, Shapur had Valerian's skin flayed and dyed before subsequently stuffing it with straw to be put on display.

Making matters worse, Valerian's son Gallienus, who was then the emperor of Rome, refused to rescue or avenge his father's death due to the sheer humiliation it brought on Valerian's family. An advisor for the first Christian Roman emperor, Constantine, wrote about Gallienus and his cowardly behavior. "Apparently Gallienus was too busy to write a letter to Shapur. Or he was too embarrassed about his father's purported footstool status."

THE PHARAOH'S DESTINY

The land of Kemet's contribution to the history of gold is still being discovered. Although long plagued by plunder and the ravages of time, the Pharaoh's destiny of gold spanning three millennia may show the world only a fraction of what's left of its stolen riches. Pharaoh Amenhotep III had more wealth than what felt like the rest of the world in eighteenth-dynasty Egypt during his thirty-eight-year reign. Amenhotep's expensive taste was similar to that of other royalty from the past, such as Louis XIV of France.

They demanded beautiful architecture. Amenhotep III built lavish monuments and temples to signify Egypt's uniformity and longevity. He inherited a wealthy kingdom from powerful pharaohs before him like his father, Tuthmosis IV. He enjoyed several years of plentiful harvests and, most importantly, gold importation. Gold was given as payment by the conquered Nubian people of Sudan.[1]

The Nile River affected all of Egypt. Its annual flooding pumped life into a desolate and dry mass of moving sand and savannah. Egypt's civilization and agriculture grew tremendously from the Nile's fertile soil, as rich mineral deposits from the river flowed north along the mountains of Ethiopia through Nubia and Sudan before spilling into the Nile basin upper-middle and lower Egypt. Mastering cultivation and animal domestication had always been a challenge for large populations, but the Egyptians mastered them.

This advantage allowed the populations to lose the concern of hunting for food and water daily instead of focusing on leisure activities, such as hieroglyphics, politics, and riches. Amenhotep used his golden fortunes to create the Luxor Temple and Colossi of Memnon, a splendor campaign that involved building large statues of himself representing the sun god Amen-Ra. Amenhotep was the grandfather of Tutankhamen, whose name meant "living image of Aten." Tutankhamen's nearly intact tomb was discovered in 1922 by Howard Carter. It was loaded with thousands of treasures, including a solid gold coffin and face mask. So, imagine the surplus of gold Amenhotep amassed in the kingdom of Egypt to allow his grandson Tutankhamen to display such wealth even in death. Mines in the eastern desert and gold deposits along the Nile toward Kush were entirely controlled by the Egyptians, who collected and smelted gold dust into nuggets.

These advanced people mastered mining the hot, barren desert terrain as the water was needed to wash gold in the mines and quench the population's thirst. Pharaohs Sety I and Rameses dug irrigation canals that allowed drinkable water across the desert, proving great care was taken to improve water supplies. The eastern desert mine produced tons of gold but little pure silver. What it did create instead was a silver-rich gold ore called "electrum," practically gold with a higher silver content ratio. The Egyptians favored this electrum, and was used as an exterior coating for obelisks and capstones for the pyramids.

Horemheb, also known as the general who becomes king, was not of the royal bloodline but a beloved advisor of Tutankhamen. His warfare and policy achievements granted him lavish gifts and gold, namely the Shebyu collar, also known as the gold of honor.[2] Timothy Green, who wrote *The Ages of Gold*, states, "As such, gold was a magic substance that protected the wearer in a hostile world. The Pharaoh also handed out honors in gold to reward his generals and officials" A forgotten pharaoh of the eighteenth-century dynasty. Horemheb moved up the ranks from a royal scribe, advisor, and war general after years of military campaigns, particularly against the Hittites and other enemies of Ay and Tutankhamen.

It was customary for precious metals to play a considerable role in the lives of Egyptian royalty, officials, and their families, who all adorned themselves in gold. Women were not exempt from displaying gold in these ancient times, and queens and pharaohs' daughters held some of the best and most valuable examples, notably Queen Nefertiti.

Three Egyptian princesses have caught Egyptologists' attention as they lay in their tombs for centuries until discovered. They were buried with gold jewelry beyond belief as Timothy Green states, "Princess Khumet's treasure was intact and spellbinding. She had a falcon collar of gold, carnelian, garnets, and green feldspar; seven rows of pendant beads connected by horizontal strings of hundreds of gold beads, all connected to two soaring falcon head terminals." During this gold age, silver was also valued by Egyptian royalty at its highest standards, sometimes more so in the earlier dynasties.

Psusennes I was a mysterious ruler and unknown pharaoh whose silver archaeologist Pierre Montet discovered coffin and treasures in 1940 after excavating several royal burial sites in Tanis. This discovery showed the excellent artistry and change in what a typical pharaoh's sarcophagus looked like during Egypt's intermediate period when the kingdom was split in two. This coffin was solid silver instead of the usual gold and is the only one ever discovered to date. A quote from Pierre Montet elaborating of his findings in the tomb goes as follows: "The treasure within the coffin was rich, with many of the ornaments showing the finest attention to detail; the fingernails carefully chased onto finger-caps of gold, to say nothing of the 36 rings on Psusennes fingers. Around the mummy's neck was a collar of over 5,000 gold discs, weighing 257 troy oz. And on his left wrist, a solid gold bracelet weighing 58 troy oz. which rather gives away the lie to any suggestion of gold shortages."

Unlike most ancient civilizations, the Egyptians were ahead of their time. Their meticulous documentation in hieroglyphics has allowed researchers to know of the infamous gold districts in cities such as Memphis. The Egyptian people would buy gold jewelry from goldsmiths, as you would see in modern-day times such as New York City's diamond district. In Egypt, gold metallurgy was nothing without the goldsmiths, who played an essential role in the culture, which used gold for adornment and worship. In Egypt, the chief goldsmiths held a high position in society, and tombs depicting hieroglyphics showed the trade's exciting anomalies. The task of making gold required skill, so the temporary gold worker was trained and complemented by the more experienced gold craftsmen in creating jewelry for Egyptian society's upper echelon.

One misconception is the amount of slave labor that occurred in Egypt to mine the gold. Many archeologists believe this information to be inaccurate or sparsely given. Yes, prisoners of war and enemies were sentenced to death, slavery, and hard labor, including mining for gold, planting crops, and maintaining temples. Still, all were not held solely for enslavement. Some captors gave reverence to the Pharaoh after defeat. Many subjects in Egypt referred to as servants or workers were most times willing to work with the hopes of moving up in Egyptian society or joining its army. They were not all held against their will.

Centuries of luxury and wealth brought events fit only for a pharaoh, such as the *sed* festival or jubilee, granted to pharaohs who ruled for thirty years or more. It was considered a joyous event that required gold, worship, and fanfare. Longevity and strength became bragging rights among pharaohs who went down in the lineage to host the most sed festivals during their reigns. In the book *Egypt's Dazzling Sun* state, Royal inscriptions state, "Amenhotep III, however, celebrated three jubilees, in his thirtieth, thirty-fourth, and thirty-seventh regnal years.

He died in his thirty-eighth year; had he lived longer, he doubtless would have celebrated more. Ramesses II, who reigned for sixty-seven years, celebrated a record-breaking fourteen sed-festivals." Rameses the Great is considered the most famous and mighty pharaoh of the nineteenth dynasty. He lived to be ninety and outlived most of his wives and children. Rameses's long reign put Egypt into a new golden age with the spoils of gold he amassed from other empires.

The pharaoh Senusret took the throne after the assassination of his father. He built the jubilee chapel made of white limestone at Karnak for his thirtieth jubilee. It is known as the white chapel because its gold and white limestone walls have high-quality reliefs etched into them, one of which depicts Senusret being crowned pharaoh by his deities Amun and Horus. Senusret became rich off his aggressive expansion in Nubia, where he quarried limestone and mined gold.

He also battled the Libyans, who were encroaching east toward Egypt's borders, a looming sign of troubled times. During the Middle Kingdom's end into the second intermediate period, gold was not always as plentiful as centuries past in Egypt. The Nubians were fierce and courageous slave troops and mercenaries for Egypt, but the tables started to turn as wars with new enemies from the west in Libya and the eastern Mediterranean added to the chaos. The Nubian people began to rebel against slavery and were no longer willing to tribute the pharaoh in gold. War with Nubia broke out, and a three-hundred-year closure of gold occupation ensued before another pharaoh could recapture the Nubian gold supply.

During these unsettled periods, tomb-robbing of the pyramids was commonplace and forced the high priests and pyramid builders to create false shafts, trap doors, and curses to deter thieves, yet to no avail. Tomb robbers plundered from burial sites throughout Egypt during these challenging times. Most were lost to history, and the people depicted as Egyptians in movies are mostly inaccurate. Egypt, and its gold, was controlled by various royal families with diverse cultural backgrounds through its 3,000-year-old history, including the Romans, Thebans, Persians, Nubians, and Hyksos.

The Hyksos were people from foreign lands, mainly Syria, who slowly integrated into Egyptian society and brought new metallurgy techniques to manipulate gold and silver. These new inventions included the horse and war chariot, and they allowed the Hyksos to join forces with the Nubians and control lower Egypt entirely.

The takeover from these foreign invaders divided Egypt into two kingdoms. It would take hundreds of years before the original Egyptian rulers could remove the alien invaders. Several pharaohs rose against the Hyksos, but it was pharaohs Kamose and Ahmose who both battled the Hyksos relentlessly, sometimes against their high priests and council's advice. Ahmose finally defeated the Hyksos and ushered in a new period of gold, prosperity, and wealth called *"the New Kingdom."* This period saw Egypt's imperial power with its complex challenges, alliances, and conquests for gold like no ancient super civilization before it.

Beyond the Nile's first cataract, the Nubian stronghold started to flex its muscles, becoming Egypt's new rival. After several years of recovering from the Middle Kingdom mishaps, Egypt was ready to expand into the Nubian territory. After the Hyksos were defeated, future Egypt's pharaohs focused their power on expeditions and campaigns to crush their enemies, and they received a shipment of gold in tribute once again, but it didn't last.

Egypt lost something more valuable than gold in both 48 B.C. and 389 A.D. the first burning of the Alexandria library during the wars with Rome and the second due to Christian fanatics, which boasted more than 400,000 volumes of books on astronomy, mathematics, literature, and medicine. Egypt would continue to defend its borders, gold, and culture from foreign invaders, ideally with the Roman towards the end and destruction of its civilization. Egypt's reign slowly came to an end, but not without amassing stories and tales about gold unmatched by societies before or after it for thousands of years.

DID YOU KNOW?

National Geographic stated in 2005 that the curse of King Tut was likely caused by toxic mold and fumes left undisturbed, then released after thousands of years. The alleged curse claimed several lives of Egyptologist Howard Carter's team weeks and months after they disturbed the coffin and removed gold relics from the Egyptian pharaoh's chamber.

The story of King Midas is a famous tale in Greek Mythology for his magical golden touch. Rewarded for helping Greek God Dionysus, he granted King Midas anything he wished, so Midas chose the ability to turn anything he touched into gold. His love for gold overshadowed everything else, and he would do anything to have all the gold the world possessed. After turning his beloved daughter into solid gold, he quickly learned a vital lesson. "Be careful what you wish for" Legend has it King Midas removed his golden gift by washing himself in the River Pactolus located in modern-day Turkey. Gold dust was abundant in the sediment of the Pactolus river, and electrum mining took place along the banks in the ancient past.

3

GOLD, GUNS & GOD-KINGS

During four and a half centuries, roughly from the years 1300 to 1750, several European countries rose to power using three things: gold, guns, and God. Gold represents the search for material gain through precious metals, slaves, trade, land ownership, spices, and other resources deemed of value. Guns refer to the superiority and destruction the Europeans advanced weaponry had on the indigenous peoples of the new world, which changed history. In this context, God refers to the missionary nature of the Spanish conquistadors who spread and converted people into Christianity violently and unwillingly.

Native peoples of the new world still believed in gold's connection to God. Rulers deemed divine, and Islam, backed by caliph gold, spread through Asia and the Middle East with astounding speed. Due to the distaste of non-Christian religions, the kings of Europe established new territories. Catholicism strengthened its position in European politics and increased its power at the expense of the landowning nobility. Conquistadors, for example, embraced the hoarding of gold in European countries to maximize their governments' wealth by accumulating gold and silver.

There was this mad dash to reach the land of milk and honey

across the Atlantic Ocean. The Olmecs already got to the Americas hundreds of years earlier, sprouting adventurous stories like one of an Afro Latina queen called Calafia who ruled on an island on the west coast of America laden with enormous gold, silver, and precious stones. *The Adventures of Esplandian* became so popular Hernan Cortés even read it while masterminding his route to the Americas. The Americas were abundant with resources igniting the stagnant economic growth of Europe.

SALT FOR GOLD & GOLD FOR SALT

In 1375, Spanish mapmakers charting the known world highlighted a particular man holding a nugget of gold above his kingdom in Northern Africa. The detailed trade routes through the Sahara Desert. The large country of Mali is located south of the Sahara Desert and has an arid terrain in the northern regions and forests in the south, called the "Sahel" by its inhabitants. A world away, Europe was rebuilding its population after the devastating bubonic plague, a bacterial disease carried by rats that caused vomiting, fever, black gangrene, and, if left untreated, eventually death.

Black rats carried this plague on merchant ships and killed an estimated 75 million to 220 million Europeans. It set the stage for the drive to identify, trade, and conquer the Middle East and North Africa. The deterioration of economic record, culture, and gold production in Europe were at their lowest, yet Africa continued to thrive.

This gold-wielding man identified for his riches went by many names, like Lord of the Mines or, better yet, the wealthiest man to ever live. It seemed to fit his description best this man was silently building an empire through gold mining and trade, and his legendary status grew year after year.

The rich African king named Mansa Musa ruled the Empire of Mali from 1312–1357. Recorded in history to be the wealthiest man in the world. He controlled numerous gold mines in a gold-rich region called "Wangara." Salt mines were also abundant in his kingdom and lured in unprecedented numbers of trade caravans and goods for commerce each year. Mansa Musa controlled the Mali Empire, which consisted of a vast network of trade routes that extended through Chad, Mali, Gambia, Guinea, Burkina Faso, Niger, and Senegal, allowing him to amass an estimated net worth of $400 billion in today's numbers, according to experts. Islam had spread from the Middle East to Northern Africa during the seventh century with Spain's Arab conquest. "Mali rulers did not encourage gold producers to convert to Islam since prospecting and production of the metal traditionally depended on many beliefs and magical practices that were alien to Islam." [1]

By the eleventh century, most Mali rulers were Muslim. Mansa never pushed his Muslim faith on the regions of the empire he conquered or visited, but he still ruled with an iron fist. Miners discovered to be thieves of gold were executed swiftly, deterring theft and kept the kingdom safe and prosperous in the gold trade. The countries in the Mali Empire had some of the most significant gold deposits in North Africa, so what the kingdom lacked in agricultural land, it made up in natural gold in the Sahel and its underground salt mines.

What made Mali and its gold trade unique was the Mali people's approach to exchange gold with foreigners for salt, silks, and camels. Unsure of the people and items traded, the Malian and Soninka empires used a silent barter system that dated back to the time of the Nubians. Timothy Green describes in *The Ages of Gold* an Arabic geographer's account of the unique gold trade process: "When the foreign traders reached the Senegal river they beat on drums to signal their arrival and set out their trade goods, including salt, and retired. The gold-diggers approached and put gold on each pile and, in turn, retired.

If the quantity was sufficient, the merchants again beat their drums, took the gold, and departed. If not, they waited for more gold until the deal was done. One would ask why trade salt for gold? Well, in ancient times, salt was more valuable than gold, mostly if you had limited quantities of it. Back before refrigeration, salt was how people preserved and flavored their foods for long periods. Knowing the Malian empire had an elaborate means of trade, you may ask how Mansa Musa earned his place on the throne.

After his brother, he came to power, Mansa Abu Bakr, who was king, read and heard stories from Arab scholars of men traversing the Atlantic Ocean to rich lands in the new world—sparking his curiosity for adventure. Mansa Abu Bakr loaded up hundreds of boats with men, food, gold, and water and led an expedition across the Atlantic to discover the Americas. Months later, only one ship from Mansa Abu Bakr's fleet returned home, with its crew detailing terrifying stories of the fleet sucked into a vast whirlpool during a storm on the open ocean.

The absence of his brother put Mansa Musa as supreme ruler in his place in the Malian Empire. He made the area a vast hub for trade, commerce, education, and economic empowerment with the help of gold. Wealthy merchants and annual Berber trade caravans had no issue paying Mansa Musa high prices for salt and gold to trade in Europe and the Southwest Asian markets. Mansa Musa made it his life mission to fulfill the five pillars of Islam. He traveled three months out of the year through the Sahara Desert, according to legend, and built a mosque every Friday.

Thus, he helped spread Islam's already flourishing religion throughout western and northern Africa without the swing of a sword or a blast from a cannon. While fulfilling his fifth pillar on his Hajj pilgrimage to Mecca, touting a colossal entourage of servants, musicians, guards, and the royal family in 1324, Musa set out from Mali to the holy lands of the Middle East. Sometimes female slaves were freed with gold or married into the Mansa Musa's royal family at caravan stops. Exquisite food was consumed, and Mansa purchased beautiful clothing at every caravan stop. As historian Edward William Bovill states, "Mansa Musa and his entourage spent much of the gold on fine clothes and female slaves, often offering five dinars where one would have sufficed."

Tens of thousands of servants accompanied Mansa Musa on his journey, wearing gold jewelry and holding gold staffs and expensive Yemini silks. Each carried a four-pound bar of twenty-four-karat gold for trade. A hundred camels carried up to 242 pounds of gold dust. Each was given to the poor as a gesture of charity along the route to Mecca. A famous quote states, "The golden rule is the man with the gold makes the rules," but Mansa Musa proved that the man who trades the gold makes the most friends. The world heard of Mansa Musa's great fortune during his 4,000-mile pilgrimage.

When Mansa Musa reached Cairo, he met with the Sultan of Mumlak, to whom Mansa Musa refused to bow, as so many before him had done as a common tradition. The sultan was not insulted but impressed at Musa's confidence, and it had nothing to do with Mansa Musa's wealth. Here stood the world's richest man humbling himself before Allah, even in the presence of the ruler of Egypt, a powerful man in his own right. Mansa Musa's extensive knowledge of Islam and the Quran was enough to have the sultan smitten with him.

Mansa Musa stated, "I only bow to Allah," and continued on his journey to Mecca. Mansa Musa passed out so much gold in Cairo, Medina, and Mecca that he caused hyperinflation, devaluing the gold currency in those regions for several months after leaving. One man's power with a vision for gold proprietorship proved that it crossed cultural politics and encouraged trade and relationships centuries before the current trade policies we have today. The allure of the gold trade turned Gao and Timbuktu's cities into centers of education, religion, and vast commerce under Mansa's rule.

The best scholars in the Muslim world and throughout Africa studied in these cities and learned from public and private libraries filled with books. Scholars held topics such as Islam, astronomy, medicine, gold, and history were held in high esteem among the people who lived there, so even today, families in Mali still keep private libraries of hundreds of books passed down from the time of Mansa Musa. They are very protective of that knowledge.

Although the Mali Empire eventually collapsed, the empires took over-utilized the wealth generated from Mansa Musa's rich past. "When Mossi raids destroyed the Mali empire, the rising Songhai empire relied on the same resources. Gold remained the top product in the trans-Saharan trade, followed by kola nuts and slaves."

Moroccan scholar Johannes Leo Africanus, who visited Songhai in 1510 and 1513, observed that the governor of Timbuktu owned many gold articles and that Timbuktu's coin without any stamp or superscription. The Mali Empire should be the main point of reference for North Africa's earlier, more prosperous age. Camel caravans still inhabited it, and blocks of salt were for sale in the markets. Concluding one story about a man named Mansa Musa, whose gold campaign helped transform a vast swath of Africa and the Middle Eastern world.

DID YOU KNOW?

The word *gold* originates from the old word *Gelo,* which means yellow.

THE GOLD FIELDS OF WEST AFRICA

At the turn of the fifteenth century, when Europeans ventured to the West African coast of Ghana, they were envious at the sight of the local chiefs of different tribes emerging from the jungles displaying heavy gold regalia and wearing Kente cloth. These African chiefs were surrounded by servants willing to assist in their every demand. According to their stories about an uncivilized Africa, these were individuals who the Europeans considered to be an aberration and no more than worthless savages.

In reality, they could not have been more wrong about the Africans, who appeared to be civilized, educated, and wealthy. Africa is one of the oldest and largest continents with gold deposits globally, a hotbed for prosperous and legendary civilizations like the Songhai and Mali empires that created wealth in these regions for centuries. The legends of Africa's diverse riches have drawn explorers, merchant adventurers, and traders from afar, forcing impromptu meetings with native people from an even more vibrant culture.

One set of people, the Ashanti of the Ashanti Empire, deep in the tropical jungles of West Africa, began as a pre-colonial Akan kingdom birthed with gold and war. In what is now Ghana, the Ashanti ruled the region from 1670 to 1957 with well over two hundred years of sophisticated culture, architecture, military power, and, most important, gold production.

The first monarch chief of the Ashanti tribe was Osei Tutu. Never far behind was his priest, Komfo Anokye. The two men organized and unified the various independent tribes of Ghana into one big nation. Osei and his people cleared large swaths of the jungle to support a growing population of Ashanti in Kumasi's capital. Going by the name Ashantene, pronounced Ah-san-ti-he-ni, meaning king of all Ashanti, Osei Tutu created a constitution and organized a military society of Akan-speaking tribes.

According to the tribe's origins, a golden stool descended from the sky and landed at the seated Osei Tutu's feet, crowning him the Ashanti ruler. Komfo was a trusted advisor to Osei Tutu, informing him this was a blessing. He confirmed the golden stool represented the spirit and soul of the Ashanti and had to be fiercely protected. Gold was not only used for adornment but also was key to Ashanti's power in the region. Alexander Bortolot, history and archaeology curator for *Columbia University*, detailed the importance of gold in the Ashanti tribe's earliest beginnings.

In his essay "Gold in Asante Courtly Arts," he explained, "Court histories state that in 1701, as Osei Tutu was sitting beneath a tree, the Golden Stool descended from the sky and came to rest in his lap, a divine gesture in support of his rule." No person was allowed to sit on the golden stool, not even the Ashantene, because it was not viewed as a functional seat but a metaphor for the Akan people's power and soul. Upholding a customary oath, the Ashantene had to pledge alliance like his predecessors to defend the truth and use gold to show his people's wealth and prosperity. He remained committed to the cause of the Ashanti tribe during his reign.

> *"An area of nearly a mile in circumference was crowded with magnificence and novelty. The king, his tributaries, and captains were resplendent in the distance, surrounded by attendants of every*

description. The sun was reflected from the massive gold ornaments which glistened in every direction." English Traveler Thomas Bowdich's dazzling account meeting the Ashanti King Osei Bonsu in 1817

Thomas Edward Bowdich, a British explorer, recounted the total shock and awe he experienced at the amount of gold witnessed at an Ashanti festival. He published a vivid description of Asantehene Osei Tutu's gold ornamentation during the first British mission to the Ashanti kingdom. "He wore a fillet of aggrey beads around his temples, a necklace of gold cock-spur strung by their largest ends and over his right shoulder a red silk cord, suspending three talismans cased in gold; his bracelets were the richest mixtures of beads and gold, and his fingers covered with rings, his knee-bands were of aggrey beads and his ankle strings of gold ornaments of the most delicate workmanship, small drums, stools, swords, guns, and birds, clustered together; his sandals of a soft white leather were embossed across the instep band with small gold and silver cases of sapphires; he wore a pair of gold castanets on his finger and thumb, which he clapped to enforce silence."

The gold the Ashanti chiefs wore was designed to showcase their power. They covered their fingers, wrists, necks, and ankles with the highest quality gold. The bright yellow metal is meant to dazzle the eye, whether on the battlefield or in ceremonies, and to provide physical and spiritual protection from enemies. When the Ashantene asserted his kingship, he did so in the most extraordinary splendor, displaying great traditional dances like Adowa and wearing gold passed down for generations.

The presence or aura of every tribal chief, starting with Osei Tutu, is believed to be radiant within Ashanti's gold jewelry, bringing power and prophecy to the wearer. The Ashanti so respected Osei Tutu that many future Ashantene adopted the name in his honor. Never alone, the Ashantene was always flanked by guards and horn blowers with gold swords, staffs, and maces and accompanied by the golden stool.

The golden seat had its private guards and remained beside the Ashantene during public events. The use of large amounts of gold regalia made sure the Ashantene stood out among the hundreds of vassal chiefs. The gold display included an Akan crown made of wood, green velvet, and solid gold castings of animals, shells, and various amulets. This confirms and shows other chiefs how precise his goldsmith's expert use of lost wax casting techniques indeed was.

Professor Edward Ayensu vividly described the tribe's gold craftsmen's capabilities in his book *Ashanti Gold*. "If the gold in Kumasi was overwhelming beyond belief, time and time again Europeans also noted with awe the quantities of gold worn in other, less rich parts of the Gold Coast. The skills and creativity of local craftsmen were widely acknowledged by European visitors, even when they were happy to melt down the jewels they had obtained to turn them into bullion." Gold and agriculture were the major commerce activities during the Ashanti Empire.

This earned the resource-rich gold coast its name. Osei Tutu made the gold mines his royal possessions, with a few high-ranking Akan chiefs having partial access to them. Artisans crushed raw gold ore from Ghanaian mines to make gold dust, the circulating currency in the empire, so no one chief could gain a massive gold monopoly except the Ashantene. The Ashanti empire had a sophisticated gold weight and scale system. Sophisticated gold weights were used to measure gold dust for exchange, and the gold artisans were revered in Ashanti culture.

Gold dust was frequently used as a medium of exchange and accumulated by Ashanti citizens of all statuses and the evolving wealthy merchant class. This elevated the social status of many in the kingdom. However, even relatively poor citizens of the tribe used gold as ornamentation on their skin and trade. It was not unusual to see lesser chiefs during yam ceremonies flaunting heavy forged gold regalia, chunky gold charms, and massive, impressive gold armlets that covered the length of their arms, in some instances up to the elbows.

Larger gold ornaments owned by the royal family and wealthier chiefs were precious and displayed their extravagance. Periodically, gold regalia was melted down and fashioned into new jewelry usually passed down from predecessor's generation after generation. Ashanti gold was essentially the tribe's primary form of economic power as they struggled for control of the gold trade with the Portuguese, Dutch, and British, who were creeping closer and closer to the gold coast's wealth of resources. The Ashanti economy doubled with the demands of the gold trade, so the Dutch were tolerated temporarily to build forts such as the notorious Fort Elmina as a place of commerce.

This allowed the Dutch to embark on business with the Ashanti—mainly to barter guns and slaves, which the Ashanti military needed to defend against their tribal enemies. The gold was mined and traded in the 1600s, and as Europeans made slavery more lucrative in the 1700s, the Ashanti sadly became a significant exporter of enslaved African people.

The constructs of slavery in Africa was very different from places outside of its boundaries. Most African slavery had no more profound reason beyond legal punishment or intertribal warfare. Europeans made it lucrative to sell slaves because, to them, labor equaled value. Gold was one of the limited items just as valuable as slaves, and intertribal warfare fueled the supply and demand.

Martin Meredith, who wrote *The Fortunes of Africa*, observed the staggering amount of slave trading, greed, and labor the British Empire profited from the Atlantic slave trade in places like West Africa before outlawing it in 1833. "British ships were the main transporters, carrying more than half the total. In the decade between 1791 and 1800, British ships made about 1,340 voyages across the Atlantic, landing nearly 400,000 slaves." These tribal wars created war captives, and those captives made slaves for barter once traders wanted slaves instead of gold.

The Ashanti had little knowledge of what happened to the prisoners after they were sold until other European nations like the Portuguese and British began building more and more slave forts along the coast. As the European numbers grew, slave kidnappings increased from the interior resulted in thousands of Africans every year getting chained up and packed into ships headed for a life of torture and hard labor in the Caribbean, Brazil, and southern states of North America.

Although it fueled some lugubrious aspects of slavery, gold played an integral role in the Ashanti trade, belief, and art. The idea of *Kra*, or the life force, is incorporated into the gold regalia via designs and symbols. Gold ornaments had a strategic purpose, as certain items were worn to tell the Ashanti people that they were at war or in times of peace. This usually coincided with the beating of drums, also called talking drums. Gold that was mined or given as a tribute to vassal chiefs from the spoils of war largely was melted down and reshaped by each chief's gold artisans, who were skilled at molding precious metal into beautiful works of art or symbols, such as *Nyame*. The symbol was considered a representation of the creator God. *Nyame* exemplifies the all-knowing power of God. Ashanti used it in gold jewelry, clothing, and artwork throughout the Ashanti empire.

The Ashantene assigned the best gold artisans to work exclusively on his royal jewelry. Working out well for the gold craftsmen because they quickly became well paid, well known, and revered. You could work for the highest bidder; all that gold accumulation brought consequences for the Ashanti, as they spent most of the seventeenth and mid-eighteenth centuries fighting off enemies to increase their empire's size and protect the gold mines they owned.

> *During the ayefor or barra ceremony, girls advertise their transformation into adult women following their first menses by sitting in public dressed in light, bright and shiny fabrics and wearing large amounts of gold jewelry. At funerals, principal mourners also wear quantities of gold ornaments, which are often hired for the occasion. The wearing of gold during rites of passage serves to distinguish and differentiate the main participants, to protect them from harm spiritually, and to redefine and reinforce the boundaries*

between different spheres and states of being during difficult periods of transition. -British Museum Curator Fiona Sheales

The Ashanti tirelessly attempted to gain control of the coastal region's tribes. The area was inhabited mainly by the Fante people and caught the attention of the British. The Fante people, a client state of Great Britain, joined the British for protection to defeat the Ashanti, with whom they were bitter rivals for decades. Backed by gold and an experienced military 80,000 strong, the Ashanti put fear in anyone who entered their kingdom in the interior of Ghana. The Danish, Dutch, and English signed a treaty of friendship with the Ashantene in the early eighteenth century to protect the interests of their forts and trade activities.

The tension between the Ashanti and outside foreigners grew larger and larger. The Ashanti were locked in disputing territory with Sir Charles MacCarthy, who assumed the position of the British governor of the Fante region at the time. MacCarthy was no longer willing to negotiate with Ashanti claims to Fante state land, and to make it worse, MacCarthy was fueled by his anger over a kidnapped and murdered sergeant by the hands of the Ashanti months earlier. McCarthy quickly assembled 2,500 armed men to confront an Ashanti army of 10,000 near the Pra River, which history will show to be a costly mistake.

Terrifying on the battlefield, the Ashanti carried the bones of slain enemies as magical charms to intimidate their foes. They painted their bodies with gold dust and war paint to ward off evil. Their army was highly sophisticated, with muscular soldiers, sword bearers, and generals wielding firearms, including the Ashantene's personal guards, and a medical faction that treated the wounded and removed the dead from the battlefield.

The Ashanti used the spoils from their gold profits to build an army that was large and menacing. After running out of ammunition, MacCarthy and his ragtag army were quickly overwhelmed in hand-to-hand combat with the Ashanti, who beat war drums and fought in the open battlefield with no fear of British bayonets.

Whether Sir Charles's courageous choice was military ignorance or arrogance, that choice cost him his life. As he was not willing to be taken prisoner fought until the end, the defeated MacCarthy was beheaded by Ashanti warriors who cut his heart out as a show of domination of an enemy and respect for MacCarthy's courage. Major Alexander Gordon, who survived, explains what he experienced on the battlefield. "A British expedition was defeated at a battle in 1824. The British were wiped out, and MacCarthy was killed. His skull and that of E. Wetherall were kept as trophies" Sporadic battles resulting in temporary stalemates caused a tug of war for several long years on both sides, with disputes over gold mines and unsanctioned crossings of the Pra River being the main components of the tension.

Sir Fredrick, a British representative, while on a visit to the kingdom years later, demanded the golden stool so he could sit on it, to make sure it was worthy enough to be entitled to the Queen of England. This caused an uproar. A battle quickly erupted that began the first of four conflicts between the Ashanti and the British army and resulted in significant casualties on both sides.

After a series of defeats, the British started to gain a foothold on the Ashanti state. After several failed negotiations in 1874, General Sir Garnet, accompanied by 4,500 British men, battled into the Ashanti capital, Kumasi, after initially meeting excellent military resistance. When they entered the city, it was mostly deserted. The Ashantene, along with his army, had fled with the golden stool into the thick jungle.

The British set every structure on fire and looted the palaces of many ounces of gold treasures before blowing them up with dynamite returning to the coast victorious. Martin Meredith, in *The Fortunes of Africa,* described the dissolution of the once-gold-rich armed society after the destruction of Kumasi: "Apart from demanding 50,000 ounces of gold, the British then left the Ashanti government largely to its own devices. Its military power had been broken. It descended into a period of internal turmoil, plagued by dissension and years of civil war."

Resentment over British occupation created rebellions led by Yaa

Asantewaa, the Ashanti people born around 1840; she rose to lead an army against the British, her son Nana Prempeh was the current Ashantene, they both battled for Ashanti rights to their land. To prop up their legitimacy as victors, the British attempted to capture the golden stool and demanded war reparations, ideally in gold, believing all the Ashanti had left was their faith and soul harnessed within the stool. The stool was sent into hiding and would remain very difficult to pinpoint its exact location, especially for the British.

The British, now frustrated with a tribe determined to preserve its integrity and not accept a proposal of protection against the French and German activities along their borders, used untraditional tactics for a victory that involved the kidnapping of Prempeh in 1896. The most impactful and victorious win for the British over the Ashanti occurred during an uprising in 1900 that led to the last and final war, called the "War of the Golden Stool."

The queen mother hated the British and would stop at nothing in eliminating them. She criticized the Ashanti men for losing morale and their Ashanti fighting spirit. After numerous defeats, the queen-mother, who once controlled her family's accession to the throne with strategic marriages, was finally arrested and exiled to the Seychelles Island off Madagascar's coast by the British in 1902.

Her capture was the straw that broke the camel's back; the Ashanti tribe was eventually defeated, annexed, and brought to heel by British forces. Yaa Asantewaa is forever embedded in Ghanaian history for being a fearless warrior who was female and a pillar of the tribe. She died in Seychelles, but her legacy lived on through her son, Prempeh. During his capture, Prempeh was chained in the dungeons of Elmina Fort, stripped of his gold regalia, transported to Sierra Leone, then finally shipped to the Seychelles Islands. In 1924, Prempeh returned to Ghana after serving twenty-eight years in exile. He reclaimed his royal access to Ashanti kingship under the British crown's watch as the Ashanti ruler.

A percentage of Britain's new gold reserves came from these colonized West African areas. Europe gained immense wealth from the trade of gold, slaves, timber, and palm oil. The region was brought into a newly annexed empire, which continued to control the gold coast as a colony until Ghana gained independence in 1957. The golden stool has not been seen by many people outside of the royal Ashanti family and only has been photographed a handful of times. In the end, the golden stool, which the British never found or captured during their colonization of Ashanti's region, remained hidden for several years.[1]

The Ashantene, also known as the Paramount chief as displayed in this illustration, reigns supreme in Kente cloth and ancestral gold regalia. The chief who stands out amongst the other tribesmen and lesser chiefs flaunt large quantities of gold as a way to impress the populace, visitors, and rivals with a show of wealth and power.

THE LAST EMPEROR OF THE LEGENDARY KINGDOM IN THE ANDES

The legend of a city filled with gold in the Andes of Peru reached far beyond South America, creating an obsession to obtain its gold a world away. Over in Europe, there were traveler's tales of huge temples people used to pray to the sun that shined with gilded gold walls and an exotic people of the clouds, wholly adapted to living in high altitudes.

These mysterious people worshipped a God-king who controlled a kingdom that stretched three thousand miles over some of the most rugged terrains in the world. "Atahualpa was the last of the native lords of the mighty Inca Empire, which spanned parts of present-day Peru, Chile, Ecuador, Bolivia, and Colombia." In the fifteenth century, Spain was on a quest to find this very mythical city of gold and its God-king, which involved sacking the new world of its natural resources.

Spain was spearheading expeditions to the new world at a feverish pace after colonizing Mexico, Panama, and the Caribbean (Hispaniola). They left a trail of carnage and infectious disease in the new world —these foreign diseases killed off the local peoples in the millions.

The indigenous peoples had no immunity against these new unknown pathogens. Matthew Hart, in *Gold: The Race for the World's*

Most Seductive Metal, explained the name *Inca*. "The name Inca refers to both the people and the leader of the empire of Peru." Huayna Capac ruled the Incan Empire and was greatly supported before his son Atahualpa took the throne.

The climb to Incan ascension was not passed on traditionally and was very competitive, causing many internal conflicts among potential successors. Huayna Capac died suddenly in 1527, most likely from a new disease brought over to the Americas. The Incan Empire had many disputes over the years after Huayna's death, such as civil war and empire expansion, but gold and silver were not one of them.

As if a lightning bolt couldn't strike twice, tragedy struck again. Huayna's heir, destined for the throne, died from smallpox as well. The empire immediately split, and a power vacuum emerged between two heirs to the throne, who were the sons of Huayna Capac.

Brothers Atahualpa and Huascar both chased the goal of becoming king or, as the Incan priests called it, the "Sun of the Sun." The two quickly became bitter rivals and caused the Incan people, loyal to either side, to stir up distrust and division.

Atahualpa controlled the empire from Quito, which is now in Ecuador, in the north, and Huascar controlled the south in the capital of Cusco, Peru. Unbeknownst to the brothers, Spaniards carrying Toledo steel swords were marching their way in search of all the gold and silver they could find. At a battle in 1532 between the two brothers, Atahualpa generals were victorious in capturing his half-brother Huascar and his rival forces. Atahualpa was known to be ruthless and swiftly killed off any loyal followers of Huascar, including local tribal leaders who could pose as a threat to his throne.

To stamp his victory, Atahualpa, now the self-proclaimed Inca, crowned the town of Cusco, the empire's new capital in the high mountains. "Their mythology tells us that they were led to build in this fertile valley by the directive of their divine creator, who gave the Capa Inca goldenrod and instructed him to build his capital city where the rod sank into the ground. In honor and reverence a sacred city was built overlooking this valley; the legendary mountain top city of Machu Picchu." [1]

Atahualpa had access to mineral-rich stretches of land in an empire reaching from the Amazon jungle to the rugged mountain peaks of the Andes in the south. Incan gold was highly abundant, and it didn't require much mining. It was easily found on the surface and given as a tribute around Atahualpa's extensive kingdom.

The Inca people had advanced knowledge of the formation of gold and silver and studied the volcanic rock geology for large ore deposits, which they have mined for centuries. Gold dust seemed to be everywhere in the river valleys, and the Inca had an inexhaustible amount at their fingertips. Only the royal Incan family and officials in government wore gold daily, as this was an item intertwined into the Inca's higher social class.

Anyone lower on the social ladder wore gold only for religious events, and those at the bottom of social hierarchy, like non-Incans and prisoners of war, wore nothing of value. Rather than as a sign of wealth, the Inca treated gold as an abstract representation of their closeness to God. The more gold worn, the closer or more blessed by God the person was believed to be in the Incan religion.

This sun-worshipping culture believed the Inca king to be the sun of the sun, so he wore the most gold of all. The temples used for worship of the rising and setting sun were covered in gold foil and plastered in red paint to worship their Gods.

Only a time machine would be able to show people in modern times the beauty of the city of Cusco, which must have glimmered in gold in the evening sun accord to Spaniard accounts. Gold was very sacred to the Inca people, and Atahualpa was worshipped as a descendant of the sun by his people like many Incan emperors before him.

Gold was the best spiritual representation of the sun's rays on a living being, which the Incans worshipped, so they shaped the gold into religious objects from beeswax molds. Since the Incans never saw gold to have any monetary value, there was a little robbery and virtually no crime in Cusco, which would later astonish the Spaniards, who stole, hoarded, and killed for a living.

Although the Inca did not record their history in written form, the advancement of their agricultural techniques allowed everyone to have access to food, such as the sweet potato. In what today would be considered a welfare state, Incan citizens helped one another in Cusco, especially the sick and the elderly; they were bathed, cared for, and fed daily. The Incans irrigated a million hectares of land in terraces for agriculture. Their system was so advanced they figured out how to stop their crops from freezing overnight.

Every day, Atahualpa was fitted and dressed in a finely made poncho with bright colors resembling the rainbow. His retainers carefully placed on his body various gold and silver ornaments laden with gems, including earrings, chest plates, bracelets, and large headdresses lined with parrot feathers. Due to the nature of the gold placed upon him, Atahualpa spent most of his days sitting on his throne under the sheer weight of the gold pieces.

While Atahualpa enjoyed his luxuries, the paved Incan roads and suspension bridges helped a new enemy journey through his empire with ease. They were already marching on a quest for undiscovered territory, mainly in the territories of the Tairona, who inhabited present-day Colombia. The Incan king heard rumors of white foreigners trading in the north but was ignorant to the fact gold was the driving force behind these men called conquistadors, and their hunger for adventure gave them the drive to press on.

Francisco Pizzaro, a conquistador, born in 1475 to a Spanish colonel father and an impoverished mother, was born poor and worked as a swine handler. He was a man of great resilience with an undying lust for wealth and adventure in a new world. "Columbus's enthusiastic report no doubt fired the imagination of the teenaged Francisco Pizzaro. Pizzaro, of course, was already well aware of the fact that his future on his native peninsula would probably be a bleak one." Francisco Pizzaro's career as a conquistador was a seasoned one by the time he reached Peru, and he had earned his stripes in central America.

Francisco Pizzaro sailed to the new world on his first expedition to the Gulf of Uraba. Gaining favor with a Spanish governor, Pizzaro has rewarded the political position of mayor of the recently colonized Panama for his loyalty. Upon hearing the good news of the golden riches his second cousin once removed Hernán Cortés had made plundering the Mexican ruler Montezuma II, Pizzaro set out to claim the Incan Empire for himself. He sailed along the western coast of South America and failed to gain a foothold on the Inca in 1524 and in 1526 due to hostile Incan natives, lousy weather, and a lack of food.

Atahualpa grew concerned as he received word from the town of Tumbez that the area was being decimated by a plague of smallpox like never seen before, and dead bodies were beginning to pile up. In 1532, Pizzaro marched once again toward Cusco, past military Incan outposts carved from ancient trees so large they resembled hands reaching to the sky. The Incan king's soldiers, many of them sick, observed him like an alien. He had a caravan of only 160 men and a few others. Most were local Indian interpreters who were enemies of the Inca divided by civil war.

Equipped with horses, guns, dogs, and a Christian priest by the name of Vicente de Valverde, the Spanish had a substantial advantage in weaponry, but Pizzaro's sheer wit on his journey would change their lives forever. Pizzaro took advantage of the weakened Incans and began to make noise as a bringer of death and the cause of havoc on the coast, using swords and guns to squash resistance.

Atahualpa knew the Spaniards would arrive in Cusco on the exact day they marched into the square as he sat on the solid gold throne he used to celebrate victories awaiting their arrival. He heard stories of the strange men traveling with strange beasts of burden called horses. Horses were never seen in this part of the new world and piqued Atahualpa's curiosity at the news of the Europeans arrival. Atahualpa, along with several high-ranking generals, controlled 80,000 Incan warriors at his command; he did not view the Spaniards as a threat.

The Spaniards arrived, but Atahualpa's mind was still preoccupied with his victory over his brother, allowing the Spaniards to camp in his empire for the night. This gesture of welcome proved a big mistake because the Spanish saw more value in the gold in Cusco then the Incans did, so they devised an evil plan to take it. Atahualpa spent the night bathing in hot springs and discussing with his royal court on his decision to kill the Indians Pizzaro had retained, castrate the Spaniards, and eat the horses. Pizzaro's brother Hernando and his men spent the night in terror, not sure if or when the Inca would attack and kill them. Pizzaro was very smart and assured his men of the plan of keeping a cavalry of armed Spaniards, led by his brother, hidden for a surprise attack.

By late evening, Incan *chasquis* runners (running messengers) informed the Incan king the Spanish were in the square hiding in a fort but were ready to speak. Pizzaro realized he would be going against a jovial Atahualpa, made friendly promises, asking the messengers to tell Atahualpa to come immediately to celebrate. The Incan king arrived hours later after enjoying numerous baths in the local hot springs, half a mile from the Cajamarca town square.

As soon as Atahualpa's feet touched the ground, a group of his loyal servants swept the square clear of any straw or debris. Atahualpa smiled, revealing gleaming green jade stones drilled into his teeth. Atahualpa wives' silver ornaments glittered and danced in the fading sunlight as crowds sang and burned Palo Santo wood incense to drive away bad energy upon his arrival.

The Inca buildings were made of large stones neatly stacked together in mind-bending positions no modern machinery or European could ever build. Atahualpa's appearance was impressive. He wore a solid-gold-and-emerald collar, and his hair was twined with a thin gold wire as he paced along the dirt path. Heavy gold rings made his swinging hands seem swollen. Vicente de Valverde emerged from concealment with an Indian interpreter and shuffled quickly toward the Incan king, who now scanned the square, shouting, "Where are they?" His comfort or, better yet, ignorance with the Spaniards showed as he had ordered most of his army to remain behind in the mountains, only bringing six thousand lightly armed men to the square.

The Christian priest invited Atahualpa to meet the Pizzaro brothers with a bible in hand at his camp hidden from view. When Atahualpa refused to be led farther, Vicente began his formal oration, a proclamation the Spanish government would state to invaders before the killing could begin. Through an interpreter, Vincente held out the bible and said it contained the life-changing faith he had been sent to deliver to the Incan people in the name of God.

The message went as follows "I request and require you to recognize the church as your mistress and as a governess of the world and universe and if you do not do this with the help of God we shall come mightily against you, and we shall make war on you everywhere and in every way that we can, and we shall subject you to the yoke and obedience of the church and his majesty." Atahualpa grabbed the book from the priest, looked it up and down with enmity, and tossed it into the bushes.

The Inca king had enough of these foreigners and scolded them for stealing from local warehouses and killing Inca chiefs. That was the signal Francisco Pizzaro was waiting for. The priest shouted, "Blasphemy! Blasphemy! Come out, Christians! Come at these enemy dogs who reject the things of God!" Pizzaro and his men began firing muskets and cannons into the crowd of Atahualpa's servants and guards from their places of concealment. "As Pizzaro was capturing the Inca, the massacre proceeded. Packed into a confined space with narrow gates, the native soldiers had no way of escape. Some thousands threw themselves against a wall and broke it down, and fled into the plain.

Spanish horsemen rode them down, lancing them as they ran and searched for any who wore the Inca symbols that would identify them." The horses stomped their hooves and whined loudly, scaring the Inca into a corral as Toledo steel and sharpened lances sliced down Atahualpa's men in droves. The more the blood flowed, the more aggressive and bloodthirsty the Spaniards became during the heat of battle. Atahualpa's most loyal servants hoisted him on his gold chair in a panic and remained with him until the end as the Spanish chopped the limbs, shoulders, and hands of the servants who held Atahualpa elevated on his throne.

In a matter of hours, the Spanish killed upward of 3,000 Inca in total. Atahualpa survived the brazen melee and was held prisoner by Francisco, who quickly figured Atahualpa was worth more alive than dead. Atahualpa, the last of the native Incan kings, now under the control of Pizzaro, still held supreme rule over the Incan people. He feared for his own death, so he ordered his military generals waiting in the mountains to stand down.

Quickly realizing gold and silver was what the Spaniards wanted, he told the Pizzaro brothers he would fill a room with all the gold they could ever want in hopes it would appease the Spanish. Locked in his prison cell, Atahualpa was in constant communication with his generals. He heard from his messengers how the Spanish were tapping the reservoir of Peru's gold reserves. Rumors quickly spread that one of Atahualpa's generals planned a surprise attack on the Spaniards for their greed and participation in the cultural loss of the Inca.

A treasure trove of gold never seen before was sacked by the Spanish. Many became intoxicated with the job of stealing gold. Mathew Hart, in *Gold: The Race for the World's Most Seductive Metal,* explains, "Some of the articles collected dated from even earlier, and showed Chinese and Vietnamese influence, suggesting that Asian voyagers might have reached Peru a millennium before the Spaniards. In a single month, they retrieved the equivalent of 1,326,539 gold pesos or about $340 million in today's money from plunder" Atahualpa's solid gold throne, along with thousands of other gold religious artifacts, was melted down into coins by the Spanish and shipped on boats headed for the Spanish mints a world away.

In 1533, rumors abounded that Atahualpa's top fearless general was approaching with a mighty Incan army, summoned by the captive Atahualpa to wipe out the intruders. The news reached Pizzaro's ears and caused paranoia and aggression amongst his men. Atahualpa never got the chance to make good on his promise to fill a room with gold as he was put on trial for treason, then sentenced to execution by Pizzaro.

Atahualpa converted to Christianity before his death to avoid being burned alive, and his body was said to have been later dug up and mummified in secret by his wives and loyal servants.2As legend goes, the location of the burial site, which hasn't been found and is said to hold the gold amassed for Spain's ransom, worth hundreds of millions of dollars, is still unknown. In the end, karma eventually caught up with Francisco Pizzaro. He met his death years later at the hands of Diego de Almagro's son, who vowed revenge for his father's death.[2]

DID YOU KNOW?

In the mountains of northern Colombia in what is modern-day Bogotá, a tribe of native people called the Chibcha performed rituals using gold centuries before European arrival. The ritual involved the local chief, who was covered in gold dust before diving into a sacred lake. When the gold washed off, it was considered a gift to the gods. Spanish colonizers who later observed this ritual called the Chibcha chiefs El Dorado or the Golden One.

MONTEZUMA'S GOLD & THE AZTEC'S BLOODY LAST STAND

Several centuries ago, a pre-Hispanic civilization was at its pinnacle on a marshy island at the foot of a mountainous valley once perceived useless and unable to grow crops. This useless valley was full of snakes but gave rise to a group of people called the "Azteca," who had such an indomitable spirit they dominated large swaths of central Mexico.

It is said the Aztec people noticed an eagle eating a snake in the middle of the lake, and the gods they worshipped deemed it to be their capital. Gold, silver, chocolate, feathers, books, and lines of captives set for sacrifice contributed to the growth of the triple alliance of the Aztec's hegemony. The sheer splendor of the Aztec cities peeked above the lush jungle canopy built over time stone by stone. Its highest reaches in their capital city Tenochtitlán were temples dotted throughout the thick vegetation.

Three huge temples—dedicated to the moon, the sun, and the last to worship the gods that connected the Aztec people to the cosmos—stuck out of the jungle environment like a sore thumb.

Spain, a royal empire in its own right, had an unquenchable thirst for gold, which gave birth to the conquistador. The conquistadors were men wild with violence and daring for adventure. Some of these conquistadors became legendary and others mediocre, but when history speaks of Hernan Cortés, the word *legendary* is an understatement.

Hernan Cortés was born in 1485 to parents with little money but a strong ancient lineage in Spain. At age fourteen, Cortés's intelligence took a toll on his parents, who could no longer control his mischievous behavior and sent him to study at a school in western Spain for gifted yet troubled youth.

Cortés grew into a fearless conquistador excited by the colorful stories of Christopher Columbus's journeys in the West Indies, of ships going into port at Valencia full of the riches from the new world. This sparked his lust for the gold that Mexico possessed.

First, he had to earn his stripes before conquering his way to Tenochtitlán, and earn his stripes he did. By twenty-six, after recovering from a bad bout of syphilis in Santo Domingo, he sailed to colonize Cuba. He was appointed clerk for Diego Velázquez, then eventually moved up to the position of mayor of the town of Santiago.

Gaining much praise and experience from being an administrator in the former colonies, Hernan Cortés had his sights set on the riches from the Yucatan Peninsula, even though he was not granted permission to start a new expedition to Mexico.

The mysterious death of a captain, plus Diego Velázquez's jealousy and distrust of Cortés's motives, caused a wedge in their relationship, which pushed Cortés to leave Cuba in haste illegally. In 1519, he amassed eleven ships, several hundred soldiers, Cuban slaves, and sixteen horses. Hernan Cortés was on his way to the Yucatan, hungry for riches in gold and a penchant for conquest.

Montezuma, the ruler of the warrior Aztec Empire, controlled his kingdom, looking for significant celestial signs from the gods to initiate ritual sacrifice and expand the Aztec rule. Severe drought and a lower crop harvest in the 1500s were believed to be a form of punishment to the Aztec people, presumed as the Aztec god's response to not being honored properly.

Therefore, Aztec rulers created wars to obtain humans for sacrifice on a massive scale in a very structured and ceremonial manner and used as offerings. Montezuma was so revered it is said no common citizen could look him directly in the eye without the threat of being punished or outright killed.

There is no denying Mesoamerica and its gold had been shrouded in mystery for centuries, so when Hernan Cortés arrived on the island of Cozumel, his mind was already set on pacifying the native Maya into not sacrificing him or his crew. He planned to obtain as much gold as possible and convert the Mayans to Catholicism.

This would be no easy feat. Yes, many of the stories of conquest involve Europeans exploiting defenseless natives of their gold and land, but the Aztec Empire was chock full of calculated warrior-like people who enslaved or killed outsiders at the drop of a hat. Hernan Cortés discovered and appointed an ex-priest, Gerónimo de Aguilar, in Cozumel, who was marooned and enslaved by Tabascan tribesmen for eight long years.

Gerónimo shipwrecked off the coast of Jamaica in 1511 on a failed exploration mission until currents pushed his rescue rowboat adrift off the coast of the Yucatan, where he made land. Many of Gerónimo de Aguilar's crew, including several conquistadors, were eaten, enslaved, or sacrificed by the natives upon their arrival onshore. Gerónimo kept his faith in Christ and claimed it to be the sole reason he was one of the lucky few used for hard labor instead of being fattened for sacrifice.

Gerónimo learned the Mayan language, customs, and culture of the Tabasco Indians and worked his enslavement debt off for eight years later before meeting Hernan Cortés and joining his crew of conquistadors, hungry to return to the Mexican mainland for vengeance. Many other Aztec expeditions resulted in failure, mutiny, or death in pursuit of the mighty Montezuma's kingdom, but the heavily bearded Hernan Cortés had several benefits during his mission that gave him the advantage he needed for victories, such as interpreters of the native language, alliances, contagious disease, and new weaponry.

Winning his first victory in the Mayan city of Potonchán, Cortés was given women, slaves, and food provisions by the defeated

Mayans. Before leaving, he sat and spoke with the local chiefs about the golden riches that lay ahead to the north. He reached the northern stretches of Montezuma's empire at Veracruz by boat.

In a feat of defiance, he ordered all his remaining ships to be burned at Veracruz's port once his men disembarked. Weaponry and provisions were unloaded, and morale was still high, leaving only two options for his expedition: victory or death.

Moctezuma (pronounced "Mock-tay-coo-schoma"), who many historians have misnamed Montezuma, considered himself semidivine and was driven by his spiritual beliefs that the stars were in alignment. He also believed the Aztec oral tradition of the "white-bearded god" by the name of Quetzalcoatl, who the Aztecs believed was due to return from the east to teach the Aztec people agriculture, astronomy, and advanced gold metallurgy.

Born in 1466, Moctezuma was birthed into royalty through his father, the sixth ruler of the Aztec Empire, who ruled until his death in 1481. The throne passed between two uncles during this time. Montezuma served as a general, gaining military experience that was necessary for him to reign later. Additionally, Montezuma had advanced knowledge of the Aztec calendar and was ordained as a priest before becoming Tlatoani, meaning "speaker" or "he who commands the people."

This position is not inherited, even if birthed into royalty but earned, and Montezuma proved himself as a capable military leader to achieve his high status. Unlike the old world in Europe, fighting on the battlefield in Mesoamerica was designed to injure and capture the enemy alive whenever possible for sacrifice later.

Aztec warriors who achieved the most sacrificial captives were promoted to the jaguar, and eagle warriors were considered the highest military honors. At this point, Montezuma's army had plenty of jaguar warriors and could easily destroy Hernan Cortés and his band of conquistadors, but Cortés was a very clever man and quickly learned as much as he could about his opponent. Through his interpreters and sheer bravery, Cortés was able to communicate with various tribes. Some were hostile toward his men, and some full of resentment for Montezuma; this resentment would eventually work in his favor.

Historian author Buddy Levy, who wrote *Conquistador*, explained how experienced in conquest Hernan Cortés truly was. In killing those loyal to Montezuma, he dismantled alliances and gained allies in the process before reaching Tenochtitlán, "The proud and independent tribe of the Totonacs, whose central city of Cempoala boasted more than twenty thousand inhabitants, had recently been conquered by the neighboring Aztecs, the Mexica. Now, against their will, they were subjects of the emperor Montezuma. Worse, they were forced to pay exorbitant tribute to their new ruler, who demanded large numbers of victims for his ongoing human sacrifices.

Montezuma had been taking their finest young men and women at will, and now he was even demanding their wives. It was too much. They no longer wished to comply, and the Totonac chief wondered whether Cortés and the Spaniards could somehow use their great power to reduce the tributes they were forced to pay.

In compensation, Cortés received gifts of gold and a massive army of native warriors from the discontented tribes, feeding his confidence to gain power against Montezuma. He agreed to help these tribes only if they could put him in the direct path of Montezuma's kingdom.

Having nerves of steel, Cortés made his way deeper and deeper into Montezuma controlled territories gaining more and more favor with tribesmen and vassals that disliked Montezuma. This where the Spanish were met with aggression; a huge clash ensued between the Spanish and the Tlaxcala tribesmen in their first encounter. Aztec weapons included the *macuahuitl*, a wooden sword fitted with volcanic obsidian glass so sharp modern-day surgeons are opting to use it over surgical steel.

The Spanish were harassed and attacked by the Tlaxcala's large numbers and fierce fighting, and they suffered their worst losses, costing hundreds of lives and several horses. Finally, the Spanish used their cannon fire to suppress and break the military lines, which finally brought the Tlaxcala into an alliance for their loss to the Spanish.

The Tlaxcala were in a constant state of war, called "the flowery wars," a state of war which they would fight but never fully defeat the Mexica and figured joining with the Spanish to topple Montezuma to end his demand for human sacrifice was their best bet to survival.

Months into his journey, Cortés and his multiethnic army—which was less than five percent Spanish comprised mainly of thousands of local natives and several hundred Afro-Cuban slaves. During their journey in the thick jungle and desert lowlands, Cortés army quickly becomes exhausted from the heat, insects, and wounds of battle inflicted by the indigenous tribes loyal to Montezuma.

Enduring a lack of sleep and exhaustion, the Spanish arrived in a town near modern-day Zautla, Mexico. Some of his men perished in the highlands from weather exposure and attacks from wild animals such as the jaguar, but he pressed on. Cortés learned intel that the Aztec's hardly fought during the night and used the night hours to cover ground. Cortés attempted to drown out the whinny calls of spider monkeys shouting from the jungle canopy and stayed vigilant.

He was well aware of Montezuma's spies trailing them. Finally, exiting from the noisy jungle, humid and full of biting insects, the dirt roads of an Aztec town became visible. This gave Cortés an eerie visual and the fear these indigenous people brought to someone who was ignorant of their religion and penchant for human sacrifice. "The skull racks, made from thousands of sacrifice victims, served as a constant reminder of their religions immense power. Human ritual sacrifice also served to bring rain and ensure harvest, as well as fertility, enacted in the feasts of the flaying of men, and the new fire ceremony."

Luckily for the conquistadors, the chief of the town received them peacefully, and many of Corté's men were surprised to witness the town's inhabitants were educated and had a strong sense of community. The chief explained the size and power of Montezuma's kingdom and capital, and this information piqued the interest of Cortés. "Most interesting were detailed descriptions of the capital city

Tenochtitlán, which he said was an impenetrable fortress on a great lake, accessible only by three major causeways containing movable bridges.

When these were removed, no one could enter or leave the city except by canoe. The city's beauty was indescribable, adding that the reach and power of Montezuma's empire were so great that over the years, he had amassed riches of gold and silver beyond imagining, much of it won in his conquests over neighboring city-states." [1] Now curious, Cortés asked a question that would change history in Central America forever.

He asked the chief if Montezuma owned much gold. A quick reply confirmed the chief said yes, Montezuma owned vast amounts. Cortés took fondness over a beautiful slave girl named La Malinche, once a daughter of a chieftain from Potonchan; after defeating them in battle, La Malinche proved to be his greatest gift in obtaining alliances and gold for the Spanish crown due to her advanced knowledge of the Maya, Nahuatl and the Spanish language.

Cortés would never have conquered the Aztec Empire without her, although in history, she is remembered as his mistress, and translator La Malinche was much more important than that. La Malinche was very beautiful and intelligent and could interpret the languages of the Aztecs, as well as Mayan, and additionally learned Spanish within several weeks of being around Cortés's men. Solely because of these skills, she is considered by some as a perfect example of treason against her native culture.

The empire of the Aztec was highly complex and advanced, with dozens of vassal states that stretched from the Atlantic to the Pacific Ocean. Yet La Malinche found a way to relate to all of them. Her ability to communicate with the fierce Tlaxcalans solidified a crucial alliance for the Spanish. She was extremely adept and could tell Cortés when she thought the natives she was talking to were being dishonest. She knew Spanish well enough to always ask for gold wherever they went.

La Malinche's insight saved the Spaniards lives many times, but once in particular, she overheard the town nobles plotting a conspiracy to kill Cortés in the town of Cholula. Upon learning of the people of Cholula's betrayal, the Spanish explorers charged the nobles with treason and sentenced them under Spanish law. The Spanish punished them in the most violent of means and sent the remaining victims to Tlaxcala for sacrifice. News of the Spaniards slaughter at the holy city of Cholula and the savagery of their fighting skills reached the valley of Mexico via Montezuma's spies, who warned that the bearded men were a few days march from the capital.

Montezuma did not approve of Hernan Cortés or his men, but curiosity pushed him to make a brash decision. Montezuma wasn't sure if Cortés was a god, a man, or something different altogether. Helpless to stop their advance in a last-ditch effort to make the Spanish go away, Montezuma sent gifts by way of his emissaries and a look-alike who claimed to be Montezuma himself to inspect and access the Spaniard's military.

All Montezuma's efforts did was feed Cortés's greed even more, as he realized there was a lot more to be had from the real Montezuma than a few trinkets of gold, chocolate, false promises, and obsidian. "The magicians and wizards, too, failed in their attempts, and the embassy returned to Montezuma with disconcerting news: all their witchcraft, spells, and conjuring were ineffective on these gods. Cortés, his cavalry and horses, and many thousands of angry natives were coming to the capital. When Cortés reached the gate of the eagle, the buildings of Montezuma's three-hundred-room palace sparkled in the midday sun like polished marble.

Some of the Aztec priests at the entrance of the causeways were preparing captives for sacrifice and wore red body paint on their upper bodies. Aztec warriors, curious about Cortés, had eagle-shaped cloaks that covered their heavily tattooed skin and jade spikes in their noses. They pointed and chatted among themselves about the strange men. Fields of crops and whole marketplaces like any modern major city encircled the marshy islands of Lake Texcoco, stunning the Spaniards with the sheer feat of Aztec agricultural engineering.

Finally, after much fanfare, Montezuma, a man who ruled an empire of twenty-five million people throughout central Mexico, met

Cortés face to face. This meeting changed the course of Mexican history forever. The premonitions Montezuma had of strange bearded men arriving on his shores claiming to the gods had arrived, but he was still unsure upon meeting them whether to kill them or follow traditional Aztec customs of diplomacy.

According to Spanish accounts, Montezuma was a sight to behold. "Montezuma wore gold-soled sandals, the jaguar-skinned thongs bejeweled with precious stones. As they came face to face for the first time, the two regarded each other. Cortés observed a man five years his senior, regal, perhaps softened from the indulgences of kingship, but lean and dark, his black hair cropped tight, his eyes piercing, deep, and meditative.

He wore a brilliant green quetzal feathered headdress and an embroidered cotton cloak studded with jewels. His lower lip was pierced with a blue stone hummingbird, his ears with turquoise, and his nose with deep green jadestone." [2] The two men exchanged words using La Malinche's interpreting skills, and a few gifts of gold was given to Cortés and his men as a peaceful gesture.

To the surprise of the band of greedy conquistadors, the Aztec ruler gave away gold without much resistance, prizing other things like jade stone and hummingbird feathers, which were used to create Montezuma's brightly colored headdress and cloak. Buddy Levy quotes Cortés first encounter "I stepped forward to embrace him, but the two lords who were with him stopped me with their hands so that I should not touch him"[3]

Montezuma softened his approach by letting his lords know he was in no danger and hoped to learn from the foreigners. He followed the customs of Aztec diplomacy, allowing the Spaniards to reside in one of his palaces for a few weeks while preparations were made for a formal meeting.

The Spanish toured the city during their stay and realized the wooden bridges leading out of the city could be removed, leaving them stranded on the marshy island if violence broke out. The finely built pyramids of the city seemed impenetrable. Cortés's conquistadors became extremely paranoid of their precarious position in the city and demanded to leave immediately in a panic, forcing Cortés to meet with Montezuma on short notice. Montezuma's brother Cuitláhuac thought the Spanish could not be trusted and planned resistance, but his ideas were disregarded by the ruler.

Cortés and Montezuma had become accustomed to speaking to one another on their perspective empires and religions during their several formal meetings, so Cortés's hasty behavior did not alarm the Aztec ruler. Once in the meeting room, thirty armed Spaniards seized Montezuma and sent his eight hundred unarmed servants running in a panic as the Spanish held him under house arrest and charged him with treason.

Using his cleverness to his advantage, Cortés said he was willing to forgive Montezuma's crimes if he gave him all the gold his kingdom possessed. Montezuma agreed to Cortés's demands, and according to legend, Montezuma gave the Spanish items from his horde, which included two gold collars, a huge alligator's head of gold, one hundred ounces of gold, birds, and other sculptures studded with precious gems, and many other priceless objects.[4]

Montezuma, now under house arrest for months, could do nothing to save his Mexican homeland and did not allow his Aztec lords to interfere with the conquistadors, who went about ransacking his palaces. The Spaniards found a secret vault so full of treasure that it took three days just to divide up the riches. Although there was enough gold to make every Spaniard on the expedition rich beyond their wildest dreams, greed became an obsession.

The Aztec people became angry at the thieves and started to question Montezuma's decision-making skills. Their treachery of impersonating the god Quetzalcoatl was finally exposed. Now led by Cuitláhuac, the people rallied and fought back against Hernan Cortés and his men, trapping them in the city.

Cortés forced the imprisoned Montezuma and his highest lord to appear on the roof of his palace in an attempt to appease his subjects from killing the Spanish. His lord shouted, "Méxicanos, your king, the lord Montezuma, has sent me to speak for him. We are not strong enough to defeat them. We are not their equals in battle. Put down your shields and arrows. Stop fighting, and return to your homes. Méxicanos, they have put your king in chains; his feet are bound with chains." Apparently, this speech fell on deaf ears. The people had enough of Montezuma's weak leadership and pacification of the Spanish.

The enraged people's fighting spirit grew, and a large crowd threw sharp stones at Montezuma, injuring the ruler gravely. No one is sure if Montezuma succumbed to his injuries from the stoning or was strangled by the Spanish, who felt he was no longer useful with Montezuma dead, Cortés and his men were forced to flee the city under very dangerous circumstances.

Tensions came to a head after the Spanish slaughtered high ranking Aztecs at a sacred ceremony dedicated to their gods. Steel and obsidian blades clashed whenever a Spanish conquistador was seen on the streets. Cortés left General Alvarado in charge, where the Aztec priests were killed. This caused the people to rebel, so uncontrollably there was no turning back for peace as the city boiled over in rage. Day turned to night, and undercover the darkness, the Spanish retreated to the wooden bridges of the city, which were now being dismantled by the Aztecs amid a full-on uprising.

Experienced Aztec warriors covered in jaguar skin pelts attacked the conquistadors any time one was spotted: Aztec spears and Spanish swords clashing in the streets. "About 200 Aztec chiefs were massacred by Alvarado's men, who were in turn besieged in their quarters by an angry mob. Upon his return, Cortés learned of the attack and uprising and quickly planned a nighttime retreat from Tenochtitlán." [5]Many Spaniards lost their newly won fortunes of gold in the chaos of fleeing in the marshy water. The greedy ones who turned back for their shiny prizes were quickly cut down with agonizing slices from the Aztec warrior blades.

The battle earned the name La Noche Triste (The Night of Sorrow). Cortés barely managed to escape with his life. He fled the city and would not return for a year. Cortés rebuilt his army and a year later returned to Tenochtitlan, which was by then further weakened by smallpox. On August 13, 1521, with the help of his Tlaxcalan allies, Cortés took back the city.

The new Aztec emperor, Cuauhtémoc, hastily tried to revive a new uprising but was captured while fleeing the city and tortured to reveal the locations of the Aztec treasure. But even with his feet held in a fire, the doomed emperor could not produce more than a canoe full of gold trinkets.

The treasure seemed to be forever lost. Cortés allowed for the torturing of any Aztec he thought might help him discover the location of the treasure. The few that were tortured stated the gold was sent north and hidden in a lake. Cortés would later search lakes in the surrounding regions to find Montezuma's treasure. He never did. The gold remains hidden until this very day.

The Aztec word for gold translated means the excrement of God's. During the night of sorrows in 1520, fighting was so fierce over the stolen gold the Spanish possessed. Hernán Cortés and his allies had to flee the capital city Tenochtitlan against enraged Aztec citizens and eagle warriors, the bravest soldiers Montezuma had at his disposal.

4
MAKE WAY FOR THE MODERN GOLD RUSH

In modern times gold and silver have evolved beyond mining for it in the ground. Its lucrative nature became the basis of most economically stable countries. Gold rushes began popping up across the globe in uncharted territories and brought swindling, horrors, wealth, and entrepreneurship for human society. The western United States has seen many gold rushes over the years as thousands of people in search of fortune pushed west to California in 1849, the mountains of Colorado in 1859, even braving the dangerously cold conditions in the Yukon Territory gold rush in 1897. The discovery of gold in the ground brought new chemical techniques to separate the gold. Many of these techniques are environmentally damaging to the planet if not stored or handled properly.

Mining for gold is a mission human beings have used throughout history to gain access to the precious metal ore hidden below our feet. Collecting quantities during a gold rush required backbreaking and, most times, dangerous work. Finding gold was not an easy task in gold-bearing regions around the planet, notably those in Africa, Australia, South Africa, China, and western America. The level of effectiveness of mining for gold quickly triggered gold rushes and hoarding. Early miners worked in a frenzy to find the mother lode quartz veins that contained the most substantial portions of the free gold deposits instead of smaller pieces found at the surface or in rivers.

The more recent gold rushes, from the 1980s to the present, increased with the influx of stock market booms and declines. New mines and advancing mining techniques were discovered that include mining on asteroids for gold ore in the future. Economic instability in 2008 and the use of precious metal in the stock market has driven human beings to demand more gold. Silver at this time moves from its mundane role of fine cutlery into a shiny metal that was given its own day in history, called "Silver Thursday," thanks to the Hunt brothers, whose greed and savvy almost controlled the entire metals market.

NATIVE AMERICAN SLAVE LABOR & ITS ROLE IN THE GOLD RUSH

They are a few scenes from the history of North America's gold rush that was missed in the history books. One of the most unknown is the oppression Native Americans endured at the hands of forty-niners and Anglo settlers looking for golden riches in California. The settlers were going into unknown territory and keeping their mining sites and frontier trails safe; a war was waged on all Indians west of the Mississippi.

Traditionally in the Wild West, Native American tribes were deemed savages with red skin running wild in the uncharted wilderness. Indian slave labor and, even worse, Indians partaking in slavery varied from tribe to tribe. Dr. Claud Anderson, who wrote *Black Labor White Wealth,* states some statistics on the matter. "These figures tell a part of the story. In 1824, there were 1,277 black slaves being held among 15,560 Cherokee's." [1] These staggering statistics did nothing to stop European settlers from enslaving Native American tribes deemed as enemies during the gold rush.

John Sutter, a Swiss-born debt-ridden shopkeeper who fled to America to avoid imprisonment, made history. "At the time, California was a Mexican province, and Sutter was tempted by its vast natural resources and its seemingly sparse population." Leaving behind his wife and children in Switzerland, he wasted little time getting his fair share of the American dream. John Sutter's smooth-talking convinced the Mexican governor of the province to acquire 50,000 acres for settlement and trade. This new land was called "New Switzerland."

Upon arrival, John Sutter quickly learned the local native people already occupied this land. A stipulation of his land grant from the Mexican government was to treat these local Indians fairly. That stipulation didn't last long; John Sutter used the Nisenan people, who were not a federally recognized tribe, to his advantage. Sutter allowed the Nisenan to work the land, but this quickly turned into a form of complete control. "Sutter told his overseer to keep his servants inline 'strictly under fear' and did not hesitate to kill Native Americans who did not submit to hard labor on his ranch. 'Sutter keeps 600 to 800 Indians in a complete state of slavery,' wrote a visiting settler, James Clyman, when he visited Sutter's ranch."

In 1848, James Marshall was hired to build a mill, and a group of Indians discovered gold on John Sutter's ranch, triggering the largest gold rush and migration of people in United States history in 1849. The role Native Americans played in this gold rush was monumental but has been tucked away from mainstream readers not willing to dig a little deeper for the truth.

John Sutter quickly took ownership of the discovery solely because it was on land he owned, but it was only half-true. "However, even the discovery of gold was facilitated by Sutter's enslavement and coercion of native peoples—indeed, Marshall was led to the site where he noticed the gold nuggets and the dirt there was dug up by a group of Sutter-controlled Native Americans who knew about the gold but did not value it."

Georgia gold was first discovered on Cherokee Indian territory in 1828, an area which later became known as Dahlonega (Indian name for "yellow money"). The federal government established a mint in the area in 1838, which produced gold coinage in excess of $6,000,000 until 1861. -Schulz

In the end, once word got out about the gold, the full brunt of the gold rush ensued as Sutter's land became invaded with thousands of settlers, miners, outlaws, squatters, and thieves. The Indians, under his control, abandoned the ranch to hold onto what little of their area they had left. Outbreaks of measles and displacement destroyed up to 80% of the indigenous populations surrounding Sutter's land. "The influx of migrants created by the Gold Rush and their excessive use of the land caused a strain on the environment; this prompted a drought and starvation took over."

The gold rush caused many hardships for both Sutter and Marshall. Sutter, up until his death, spent every dime he had fighting the United States government for restitution and Marshall giving his best years as a failed gold miner. The bitter truth is the Native American's knowledge of gold on their lands and the hard labor they endured brought about the California gold rush, and it would not have occurred without them.[2]

DID YOU KNOW?

African Americans and Native Americans were denied access to gold during gold rushes by local laws and white vigilante violence. The difficulty to freely pan in a discovery that after only four years extracted a value of $200 million in gold profits stifled wealth among these two racial groups.

HOW ELECTRONIC WASTE DUMPS ARE BEING RECYCLED FOR PRECIOUS METALS

Since the introduction of plastics on a mass scale in the 1950s, communities have used recycling as a means to cut back on waste and humanity's carbon footprint. Landfills across the globe are loaded with cell phones, televisions, laptops, and other electronic waste full of plastics and harmful chemicals.

This waste is usually dumped in third world countries, out of the sight of wealthy Americans and Europeans. These mass mounds of electronics hold something much more valuable than plastic; gold is in abundance as well.

A *Time Magazine* article explained how corporations are looking to the future of gold mining in electronic waste dumps. "Japanese company Mitsubishi plans to invest about $108 million to expand operations to sift through discarded computers, cell phones, and other electronic devices to recycle rare metals such as gold and palladium as global supplies dwindle."

The inner workings of these electronics are full of heavy metals that are valuable, and recycling them is safer on the environment than traditional mining. Gold has only a limited supply; mining for it in landfills has become a new form of a gold rush. Let's face it: with climate change, a hot topic in the media, gaining recycled gold while helping Earth's environment is a two for the price of one type deal.

The project leader of a cellphone recycling company called *Closing the Loop* breaks down how he plans to create a different approach to electronics, gold, and recycling. "Around two billion mobile telephones are sold around the world each year.

Only half a billion are reused or recycled, while the rest end their life contaminating the earth in countries with unsafe and unregulated recycling practices, in illegal landfills, or just hanging around in drawers. These 'junk phones' don't just lead to health and environmental problems. They are also a waste of valuable raw materials in a time when access to tech is still not for everyone." 1

THE IRISH SILVER KINGS

One of the largest silver beds ever found is in the state of Nevada. Once settlers discovered silver there, people flocked from every corner of North America to get a piece of the pie. Four men looking for fortune created an alliance to buy silver mines and invest in silver-mining shares. Jack Mackay, James Fair, James Flood, and William O'Brien are known as "the Silver Kings." In 1871, the four Irishmen consolidated Virginia Silver Mine near Virginia City, Nevada.

Starting slow, they bought small claims on the infamous Comstock Lode and later the California mining operation in Virginia City. What made the Silver Kings unique was Jack Mackay, and James Fair had mining knowledge, and Flood and O'Brien had wealth. The accumulation of the mining share claims over time produced a bonanza of wealth. Gold caught the buyers' attention, but the sheer amount of silver in the Comstock Lode made quite a few men such as these four richer than most gold miners who struck it big.

By 1875 the Silver Kings had become extremely wealthy. Consolidated Virginia was paying monthly dividends of a million dollars, equivalent to 20 million in today's dollars. From 1873 through 1882, Consolidated Virginia yielded some $65 million in gold and silver and paid almost $43 million in dividends. -Dr. Roger D. McGrath

O'Brien, Flood, Fair, and MacKay rode the silver rush wave to the very end. After the Comstock Lode depleted, these ambitious go-getters investing their wealth from silver into other avenues of revenue. O'Brien supported all his close relatives and left an estate worth $12,000,000 at his death. Flood bought real estate in San Francisco and created the Nevada Bank, which later would become Wells Fargo.

Fair lost $5,000,000 to his wife in a divorce, became a senator, and still managed to pull $250,000 a month in rent from tenants and establish two banks. Mackay's estate was worth $50,000,000, making these men the true kings of silver.

THE WORLD'S DEEPEST GOLD MINE

Gold mines cover large portions of the planet in places like Brazil, the Democratic Republic of Congo, and Australia. Still, the depth to go underground at the Mponeng mine is a feat humankind had never achieved. Gold is so sought after by humanity that people are willing to do anything to get their hands on it, including drilling deep into Earth's center.

In South Africa, the Mponeng mine is a hole cut 2.5 miles into Earth's crust, allowing miners to tap into the largest gold-retrieving metropolis in the world. The mine seems to operate on a risk versus the reward system. It is full of tunnels reaching two hundred and thirty-six miles long, and the extreme heat, earthquakes, and poor ventilation pose major risks to the well-being of anyone entering the expansive mine. Still, the value of the gold it possesses is a worthwhile reward.

Journalist *Matthew Hart* who visited the mine in 2012, explains the risks of mining for deep gold underground creates. It seems even in the event of an emergency if you make it to the caged elevators that allow you to reach the surface of the mine, new dangers await. "The hoisting apparatus for a cage that carries people instead of rock is called a man winder.

Sometimes it winds men to their death; on May 11, 1995, in the Vaal Reefs gold mine, ninety miles south of Mponeng, an underground railway engine broke loose. Pulling railcars after it, the engine plunged 7,000 feet down a shaft onto a two-deck cage, killing the 105 men who were returning to the surface at the end of a shift."

Exactly how much gold could the world's deepest mine be producing to encourage people to risk their lives in a place that can get as hot as 140 degrees Fahrenheit? A lot. The gold-mining industry has put up some promising numbers in many sectors, although gold output from mines worldwide is declining.

This is Gold; a company created to give insight and initiative on the gold-mining industry is a great resource. In South Africa, amid increasing costs, the organization explains gold mining is still lucrative. Mining contributed $42.7 billion to the economy of South Africa thanks to gold. In US dollars, that's about $3 billion if you're not factoring in inflation. December 2016 saw 138 tons of gold bars produced from the mine alone; now that's a lot of gold.

Security guards also tend to let these ghost miners be: the illegal miners armed with AK-47s and beer bottle grenades, and it's all too easy to hear someone coming from far in the mine. The mine is so big; it's difficult to police anyway. There's also a whole, well, an underground economy where legal miners help out their illegal brethren. For example, since bread costs twelve times as much in the illegal economy, packing some extra lunch can get you much more than lunch money.

The richest gold source in the mine is a vein of ore attached to the bedrock that is only thirty inches wide. That's small in comparison to the amount of digging it took to get there. Each day miners will be extract gold from these thirty inches of ore until it runs dry. The price of gold is just as volatile as the rock it is lodged in. I would imagine miners must feel like they are extracting gold coins from underneath a sleeping dragon.

Super-heated rock bursts can suddenly shoot out scalding shards of water heated stone that can maim or kill miners. While these rock bursts are present in most commercial mining operations, they are commonplace in deeper mines because the deeper you go, the more it requires to keep the mine intact against the forces of pressurized rock. The looming reality of running out of gold soon is forcing miners to dig deeper and deeper.

Journalists Alexandra Wexler and Thandi Ntobela of the *Wall Street Journal* show the scary price many miners face trying to provide for their families. "Gold at these depths is costlier and more dangerous to mine. In South African mines, deaths rose for the first time in a decade last year, climbing 21% from a year earlier. So far in 2018, sixty-five workers have died, including twenty-four deaths at Sibanye Gold South Africa's largest gold producer." [1]

Unskilled and uneducated miners working deep in the most dangerous portions make up a large percentage of the deaths. A lack of technical skills plays a role in the world's deepest mine's decline in production and employment. In the past, apartheid played a huge role in cheap mining labor, but times are changing.

Residue from that trying period in South Africa's history is still prevalent among mineworkers who demand training and education in the mining sector. Nick Holland, the chief executive for the Gold Fields mine, told the *Wall Street Journal,* "We are training a lot of people in the classroom, and the training facilities are getting some good results, but our ability to translate that into the workplace is somewhat absent." The company also said it expects to let go 1,100 employees and about 460 contractors at the mine, or about 28 percent of its workforce, as part of a restructuring.

Even with the doom and gloom involved in deep mining, discoveries in mining technology and biology are still being made. Scientists have discovered organisms living in the dark depths of the Mponeng mine. Maybe these organisms, called "extremophiles," can be viewed as a symbol of the determined miners' spirit.

An article from the *Wall Street Journal* states how these microorganisms feed on the same precious metals the miners are drilling for: "Scientists now know that so-called extremophiles—microorganisms that live in acidic or hot environments—are common and that they also thrive in ultra-frigid places. They can survive high radiation, too, and feed off or breathe metals, like uranium or iron.

The rod-shaped bacterium lives alone in the dark, hot waters of Mponeng; it is the sole member of the only single-species ecosystem discovered. All life forms need basic nutrients like carbon, hydrogen, nitrogen, and, usually, different bacteria pull different nutrients from the environment to form an ecosystem. But the bacterium is self-reliant, capable of producing everything itself. Scientists think the bacterium has not seen the surface of the earth in millions of years.

The lowest parts of the Mponeng mine being excavated can be accessed only by foot. Anglo Gold Ashanti, the third-largest mining company globally, plans to sustain the Mponeng mine's life longer with new expansion plans and $1 billion in funding. Mining.com sees a bright future for the mine once they keep digging deeper into new portions of the mine's gold-rich ore. "The new approach, which optimizes the project as a whole, is expected to set up Mponeng as a producer of 450,000 ounces of gold for more than 20 years, with all-in sustaining costs improving to about $750 an ounce."

The future of the world's deepest mine seems to be in the hands of men and women who are willing to risk it all for new sources of gold. The Mponeng mine extracts 6,000 tons of rock per day but needs to extract only 0.35 ounces from one ton of rock to profit. Massive earnings like this are a tribute to gold's worth. Digging to Earth's center has passed insanity to reality.

THE MAN WITH THE $250,000 GOLD SHIRT

A surefire way to make headlines and jealous enemies in the same setting would be to wear a custom shirt stitched with 14,000 pieces of twenty-two-karat gold. Indian businessman Datta Phuge bought the seven-pound shirt for 12.7 million rupees, or $240,000, in 2013, earning him the name *"Gold Man of Pimpri."* Datta's love for gold overwhelmed his fear of flaunting it so much in public, a decision that cost him his life. The man with the gold shirt was determined to make history, not receive envy.

"Everybody knows me as the 'gold man' in the whole region. Other rich people spend one crore (10 million rupees) to buy Audis or Mercedes, to buy what they like. What crime have I done? I just love gold" –Datta Phuge.

The shirt was so outrageously expensive it earned Phuge entry into the 2013 *Guinness Book of World Records* for the most expensive shirt. Phuge ran businesses in cooperative credit, money lending, and other financial markets, so coming up with large amounts of cash to purchase it was easy. Avoiding the jealous eyes and hatred for your wealth in a country with 23.6% of its population living off less than 1.25 dollars per day proved impossible.

Accordingly, I picked up the food and arrived at the spot, anticipating that the birthday celebrations would have started. However, I saw that around twelve people had surrounded my father and were attacking him with sharp weapons and stones to my horror.

I started shouting and ran towards them. By that time, my father had already collapsed. Even as I ran towards them, one of the attackers picked up a huge stone and smashed it into my father's face. Then, they all ran away. When I reached my father, it was too late." –Shubham Phuge.

On a dark Thursday night in 2016, Datta Phuge and his twenty-two-year-old son Shubham were invited to a birthday party held by some of his son's friends. This where things get strange: at some point on their way to the party, Mr. Phuge's son was told to pick up food and two packs of cigarettes. Datta Phuge decided not to wait and went ahead to the party without his son. When the son arrived, he witnessed his father being dragged from his vehicle and sliced with a sickle, stabbed, and bludgeoned with large stones.

According to his son's accounts, Phuge was not wearing his famed gold shirt at the time of the murder. Shubham admitted he thought the men who attacked his father were friends but now believes the suspects had a contract to kill Datta Phuge. Several bodyguards usually accompanied Phuge, but he did not have any with him that fateful night. Strange, but it's a true story.

5
THE ESOTERIC VALUE OF GOLD & SILVER'S MYSTERIOUS HEALING POWER

Long ago, man considered gold and silver to possess magical, esoteric properties, and the enlightened who used it correctly could gain spiritual enhancement, healing power, and strengthened internal vibration. A lot of this knowledge naturally has been lost through time, and there is limited research on exactly how gold and silver can benefit the physical body when handling or in close contact with it.

These metals' true value manifests only once individual returns to living in union with the body and removes gold and silver from the ranks of money or social status this is when its metaphysical powers become auspicious.

The yellow metal has been used to uplift well-being when found in its purest grades. Gold that has been alloyed or mixed with other metals will still work but is less effective. Silver ore has been used in the past to bring in a purifying light and reflection into a person's life, which is why people commonly used to make mirrors using silver.

The high priests of Egypt were known to ingest gold for mental and spiritual purification, as they believed that gold strengthened the life force, removed disease, and raised the body's vibration on all levels. Silver is symbolic of strength because of its resistance to high heat and pressure. It can be molded into any desired form and resonates with healing lunar energy.

These benefits were intended for a limited few to understand the power of gold and silver. Many cultures, such as the African, Chinese, Indian, and Persians, have adorned themselves for centuries with precious metals and gemstones to achieve higher positive energy levels during prayer and meditative states.

When working on strengthening spirituality, gold is an essential component for a human to operate at a higher frequency for divine consciousness and soul liberation. According to some studies, Gold is known to open the crown chakra, which helps gain enlightenment and make sound decisions. The pineal gland is revved up to a higher spiritual development when gold is placed on the body. Gold's powerful effect is very subtle but very apparent once worn.[1]

DID YOU KNOW?

King Solomon's legendary "lost" gold mine, which yielded much of the Kingdom of Israel's fabulous wealth nearly 3,000 years ago, may have been found. According to the Bible 1,086 talents, or about 34 tons of gold were brought to Jerusalem by Solomon's workers. This quantity, worth about $125 million at today's prices, is thought to have constituted about half the ancient world's known gold supply.

GOLD: METAPHYSICAL PROPERTIES & POWERS

In today's world, people rarely comprehend the real value of gold's metaphysical power. The truth is gold allows you to be more aware of what should hold value in your life, such as realizing that mastering your inner golden self is more valuable in the long term than making money from gold in the short term.

Although gold can provide both when used on an esoteric and a physical level, it works best for igniting conscious wisdom, making you wonder why kings and queens wore gold crowns and held gold scepters. Gold's secret is, the more you are in contact with it, the brighter you become.

Beyond the bling factor, a heavy gold crown placed on a ruler's head may have helped him or her decide what was best for the kingdoms they commanded, a result of gold's purifying, balancing and revitalizing energetic nature. A solar metal, gold can be used as an energy shield when exposed to the sun's heat. It can deflect radiation on various levels, which NASA has recently exploited to prevent radiation damage to its spacecraft.

In ancient times, people wore lots of gold daily for happiness and spiritual peace, and in today's eastern cultures, it is still used similarly.

The ions in gold possess supernatural warm energy that stimulates strength, power, and loss of energy flow within the body.

Since gold is a warming metal when in contact with the body's aura and energy fields, it is usually worn on the body's upper parts, such as the neck, wrists, ears, nose, and fingers, for maximum results. According to Vedic tradition, gold is worn below the navel negatively charges the body, causing a mental disturbance, lack of sleep, and disruption of the body's heating and cooling.

Gold is beneficial in attracting prosperity, respect, and wealth into your life. Ensuring readers would be given the most authentic insight into precious metals' mystical properties in connection with metaphysics and esoteric energy. I studied a wide range of information that contained comprehensive knowledge on the properties of the mineral kingdom. According to *Love is in the Earth: A Kaleidoscope of Crystals,* here is a list of gold's beneficial properties used as a healing mineral on the body. The information given is purely metaphysical and is by no means medical.

•Gold helps to improve one's character via learning, lessening the trauma associated with situations experienced during knowledge gain. It assists one to activate, to mobilize, and to actualize the intrinsic potential of the self.

•The energy of gold can be used to balance the energy fields and assist one in eliminating ego conflicts and feelings of futility. It can also help to assuage the overburden of responsibility, combat feelings of depression and inferiority, and allow one to both understand and dispense with self-reproach, from excitation and states of anger.

•Gold has been used in the development, purification, and balancing of the heart chakra and amplifying thought-forms. The purity of gold is said to help one to preserve higher thought forms for later retrieval.

•Gold has also been used to open and to activate the third-eye and crown chakras. It has been said to attract honors, wealth, and happiness, to provide composure, to balance the emotional system, to alleviate tension and stress, and to amplify positive feelings. It also assists one in attuning to nature and its healing forces.

•It can clear negativity from the chakras and the energy fields of the physical, emotional, intellectual, and spiritual bodies while transferring the vitality of any companion mineral to the affected area. Gold produces an energy that is both cooperative and receptive, allowing for extensive use with other gemstones; it is capable of attracting and maintaining those qualities which are inherent within the additional stone. When in proximity to another mineral, gold provides a balancing influence on the energies of that mineral.

•Gold has been used to enhance mental faculties, rebuild the nervous system, and treat multiple sclerosis, improve digestion, circulation, and breathing, and increase warmth. It can also be used to treat arthritis, skin cancer, blood disorders, pneumonia, vascular diseases, heart disease, eye problems, paralysis, rheumatism, skin disorders, tuberculosis, nightmares, and spinal problems.

•Gold assists in rejuvenating the endocrine system, in the absorption of vitamins and minerals, and in the regeneration of tissue and the skeletal structure. It balances the right and left brain, and treats conditions associated with autism, dyslexia, epilepsy, and physical coordination.

Gold and silver are transformative metals that can form an invisible barrier against electromagnetic radiation around the wearer's energy fields. It is highly recommended to keep these metals clean and shiny at all times. Gold and silver jewelry should be cleared of negative energy with sage smoke and kept extremely clean as gold can easily become a collector of negative energy over time. What makes gold and silver unique metaphysically is they are good conductors of electricity. Wearing them can help in transmitting electrical signals throughout the body.

Mixing gemstones with gold, like emerald, ruby, turquoise, and diamond, increase the gemstone's strength. Think of it this way: gold and silver are great conductors of solar and electrical energy, and the gemstones amplify that energy tenfold. Outside of their sheer beauty, gemstones like diamonds are mineral carbon crystals that manifest and absorb unique vibrational energies, similar to the way gold absorbs photons from the sun, strengthening the confidence of the wearer and warming the spirit.

Has anyone thought about why we wear gold rings to symbolize marriage? According to most cultures' traditions, the belief is an artery runs directly from the ring finger at an acupuncture point on your left hand straight to your heart. Could the divine benefits of wearing gold as a symbol of love keep your heart healthy and heal wounds on the body? Possibly, but that is still up for debate.

It was considered that gold relaxes the body's restricted blood vessels and encourages new cell growth. Among those in the healing and jewelry arts, this possibly transcended into gold ring symbolism.

Gold is known to heal the body of aches and pains and never tarnishes; when we want to show our fondness for our partner visibly, a gold ring is placed on the left ring finger to represent an untarnished eternal marriage or committed engagement. Couples who are experiencing problems getting pregnant have a better chance of doing so if they wear gold rings on the wedding finger.[1]

This yellow metal helps the crown chakra to open, giving gold a masculine energy that governs the wearer to uplift their spirit. Feng-Shui is one of the five arts of Chinese metaphysics and can be increased if you keep gold in your home, with both the color yellow and physical gold tucked away in a room. Gold that is gifted to someone near and dear encourages prosperity for both parties. When worn externally, gold can be very beneficial to your aura as it draws the laws of wealth and attraction to the wearer, and your spirit will have a better understanding of its sense of duty.

Gold is connected with all the planets in astrology but mainly the Sun and the planet Jupiter placement in your horoscope, making gold more beneficial for specific natal charts and astrological signs over others. For example, Leo, Cancer, Aries, and Sagittarius benefit from wearing gold, whereas Pisces, Virgo, Taurus, Aquarius, Scorpio, and Gemini can have varied results. Capricorns and Libras should avoid wearing gold due to the possibility of it giving bad energetic vibrational results. Wearing silver for these two astrological signs is a better option and will strengthen them similarly to the way gold does for other signs in the horoscope.

In general, wearing gold should suit everyone, but it isn't always beneficial for every person. According to legend, if gold does not suit you or a person doesn't follow the rules of gold while wearing it can bring bad luck, ill health, and a loss of prosperity. Gold should never be bought if you know it's stolen or sold with ill intent.

Like most things in the universe, gold is governed by a set of karmic rules. Stealing gold will bring wealth at first but has claimed that it later can create problems, financial loss, and administer negative karma in the lives of people who do not follow the rules of gold while possessing or trading it.

DID YOU KNOW?

Anyone can use gold as a jumper wire that allows the energy to go from one meridian that is normal and strong to weaker and not functioning. It gives power to the weak or shocked meridians. Thus, it helps the body to heal itself in many respects.

SILVER: METAPHYSICAL PROPERTIES & POWERS

There will always be naysayers claiming silver does nothing to benefit the body, and the power it administers is hocus pocus, but they are misinformed in that regard. In folklore, silver had many uses, including channeling magic, amplifying precious stones, and turning water into a healing elixir of sorts.

Silver is very reflective of light, much like the moon is reflected in the night's sky. Silver gives a magical calming effect to the wearer when worn on the body when under stress or around infectious pathogens. Silver's power is linked to the lunar and feminine energy that helps with communication, physical ability, and emotional balance.

When used in the correct manner, silver cools the body and protects against electromagnetic radiation. Usually, silver jewelry is worn on the lower parts of the body, allowing it to harness the moon's energy easier.

Silver ornaments worn on the ankles prevent knee pain and backache. Its resistance to high temperatures makes silver a great conductor. It is used in almost every electrical application as well as in batteries, switches, and coatings.

The astrological signs powered by the moon, such as Cancer, Aquarius, Libra, and Capricorn, can see a benefit in wearing the silver medal. Also, those who are vulgar or in need of detoxing high levels of negative energy or illness can achieve betterment in these areas by the power silver brings forth from the universe.

Silver has been used for centuries for its antibacterial properties, incorruptible pureness, and protection from magic and evil intent, wildly used by magicians, palm readers, vampire slayers, and alchemists alike. Silver has mystic powers and is akin to its nobility to gold. When used together, it can create a sense of divinity.

Silver's power is shown in its scientifically proven ability to kill everyday germs and bacteria on the body, especially while traveling. When silver is left in pitchers of unclean water, doctors noticed it cleans and creates scum-free silver colloidal water, which some belief is alkaline, healing, and free of all impurities. Colloidal silver water usually contains pure silver ion particles suspended in demineralized water, which kills bacteria and viruses.

Colloidal silver was a preferred choice by physicians in the 1930's and 1940's before the advent of antibiotics. Colloidal silver, when ingested, kills germs and builds immunity but can also cause serious side effects if over-concentrated or created by an inexperienced alchemist. The most common effect is a bluish-gray discoloration of the skin, which is usually permanent. It can also damage the thyroid in high doses. Silver jewelry is alleged to provide security against magic and to enhance the connection between the psychic link and the wearer.

The information given is purely metaphysical in nature and is by no means medical. Here are some other little-known facts that can occur while harnessing silver's esoteric power, according to *Love, is in the Earth: A Kaleidoscope of Crystals*.

•Silver brings "the advantage" throughout life. It can be used to improve one's quality of speech and can bring eloquence to conversations. It tends to bring an air of culture to one's presence and to eliminate abrasive traits while promoting popularity.

•It can draw forth negativity from the body while transferring the positive forces of the other minerals; hence, it performs as a balancing agent.

•Silver helps to cleanse the body via the pores and to eliminate toxins at the cellular level. It can be used in the treatment of hepatitis, to increase the assimilation of vitamins A and E, and to ameliorate disorders associated with unstable vision.

•It is known to enhance the powers of the moon and excellent mineral for use in energizing other stones during the full and new moons.

•Silver is used extensively with gemstones because the metal is able to both attract and retain, unto itself, those qualities which are emitted by the stone.

•It can be used as a mirror to the soul, one to simulate seeing oneself from outside of the body. This sight is without judgmental altitudes and can provide for a stepping stone to the furtherance of that which the I Ching recognizes as the "superior man." It provides one with patience and perseverance in the tasks chosen and allows one to understand the underlying reasons for the tasks. It assists in increasing perception and helps to regulate the emotional and intuitive energies.

Human beings are connected to these metals with a mysterious magnetizing attraction; the healing properties of gold and silver have been exploited by master healers, shamans, oculists, alchemists, and royalty for centuries. Precious metals have helped them achieve "all that is" and "the advantage," a spiritual, metaphysical frame of mind man has chased since opening Pandora's box.

Using these precious metals on the body hasn't been proved scientifically, but to so many, it assists in overall well-being and spiritual growth. The remarkable benefits of gold and silver are subtle but slowly but surely being rediscovered, as today's scientists uncover what the ancients seem to have known all along: gold and silver are indeed mighty esoteric precious metals.

DID YOU KNOW?

Babies under three months have more traces of gold in their hair than older people. The gold comes from their mother's breast milk and can reach double the average concentration of gold in the Earth's crust.

THE FORGOTTEN LAWS OF GOLD

Wearing gold on various parts of the body has been a tradition by people worldwide for a long time. During that long history, the do and don'ts while wearing it naturally accumulated generation after generation into modern times. Drinking alcohol or eating a non-vegetarian diet while wearing gold can negatively impact you.

Gold helps those that own businesses or have an entrepreneur mindset prosper, but if your business is related to the iron or coal business, don't wear gold. In the Hindu religion of Veda, gold represents Jupiter and the Sun, and those who wear it should try to maintain a positive way of life as gold is considered a divine metal worn by the divine. These laws or rules about gold are up for dubious debate but are nonetheless exciting and maybe wouldn't hurt to give it a try.

People should wear gold with other real jewelry, and the wearer should never wear artificial jewelry with gold or keep it mixed in with non-gold jewelry while in storage. All different kinds of jewelry should be kept in a separate place from authentic gold jewelry. Certain personality traits may hinder your ability to wear gold, such as impatience, anger, and being too loquacious.

Pregnant women should avoid wearing a lot of gold, or if they are real gold lovers and severely attached to it, should wear less than usual. Silver is a better metal to wear during pregnancy. If your house in Jupiter is in a lousy placement on your natal chart, like the 6th, 8th, or 12th house, you should avoid wearing gold.

Never accept gold if gifted by an enemy. Gold should be kept in red color clothes, or bandana's when not worn, and older adults should not wear too much gold due to its weight on the physical body in large quantities. The laws of gold are a set of instructions with unknown origins from a golden age spread around cultures worldwide.

As a symbol of authority, gold in the past and present requires a level of confidence to maintain and safeguard. So, next time you wear your gold jewelry, following some of these laws that may benefit and allow you to have a more enjoyable experience when adorning your body with the yellow stuff.

THE GOLDEN BABA OF INDIA

Gold in India has a long history with the Hindu religion. Those looking to enhance their spirituality can use gold to amplify their blessings as well as their savings. Indians hold more private gold among its citizens than Americans, Swiss, and Germans put together.

So, researching Indian holy men, called "*babas*," wearing extreme amounts of gold on their body for healing and sacred divinity wouldn't be hard. There are many godly men in India. Some wear gold, and some don't, but the golden *baba* has to be number one among the ones who do.

His real name is Sudhir Makkar, but his fascination with gold earned him honors of being a living saint among many followers. The "golden *baba* makes his appearance once a year during the Kanwar Yatra pilgrimage. During the Yatra, millions of devotees of Shiva travel miles to sacred lands to fetch holy water from the Ganges River.

During this journey, the golden *baba* can be found donning up to 20 kilograms of gold jewelry on his body, surrounded by five bodyguards and hundreds of followers touching his feet for blessings and jostling for position to see the older man with the gold.

Before taking up spiritualism, Makkar ran a successful cloth and property business in Delhi. Makkar adds more gold each year he attends the Yatra, and in 2018 he had participated in twenty-five thus far. The gold is a clear indication of his devotion to Shiva, which he believes has blessed him and allowed his business to flourish.

There has been some controversy that Makkar was a criminal earlier in life and became a holy man to avoid charges. When the golden *baba* was asked why he is so obsessed with wearing gold, he stated, "There was a time when I used to wear only a few grams of gold, but with Shiva's blessings, I am now wearing gold in kilos. It's so heavy, you will not be able to hold it," he shared.

The *baba* said he would continue to add gold for every pilgrimage he attends until his death; then, he plans to pass down the gold to his most loyal disciple. Thanks to social media and cell phones, the golden *baba* has become very popular in Indian culture.

There are several articles and videos of the *baba* parading around in a caravan using the law of gold's attraction to his advantage. Whenever he can, he returns to the community and receives gold as a reward from his followers. Hopefully, we get to see many more years from the Golden Baba. Maybe next year, he will show up to the next Yatra with forty kilograms of gold.

DID YOU KNOW?

According to Irish legend, leprechauns love gold so much they are known to carry one gold coin for every year they have been alive. Not all leprechauns are mischievous; some people lucky enough to capture a Leprechaun can trade their freedom for its treasure. Leprechauns are usually said to be able to grant the person three wishes.

THE SILVER POTION THAT TURNS MEN & WOMEN INTO X-MEN

In 2017, *Wired Magazine* covered an article on a blue-skinned man named Paul Karason who shocked the world in 2008 on the *Today Show* with his unusual skin and addiction to drinking water laced with silver ions.

Far removed from the Hollywood big screens, this unique look Karason had is a medical condition called argyria, a discoloration of the skin and mucus membranes that can give the person afflicted a bluish-gray tint from silver exposure. I'm sure most people would not subscribe to having their skin look like Beast from X-Men, but most taking unregulated silver supplements don't realize until it's too late.

Some people have been prescribed colloidal silver's healing tonic for decades without knowledge of silver buildup in the body. Rosemary Jacobs developed blue skin after being prescribed nose drops containing silver at age eleven. Rosemary was subjected to teasing, difficulty receiving employment, and never a long-term relationship due to her strange skin color. She has spent 60 years of her life trying to raise awareness of silver in dietary supplements and how the condition can ruin a person's life.

Karason bought a device to make his colloidal silver at home—a colloid is one substance dispersed through a second—and soon he was drinking a 10-ounce tumbler of the stuff daily, hoping to improve his general health, and dabbing it on his face for his dermatitis. -Mallory Pickett

Advertisements and supplements claiming silver's immune-boosting benefits were based on scientific proof but risky. Many silver enthusiasts that produced colloidal silver at home had no way to predict the number of silver ions leached into the product.

Thus, the chances of argyria increase significantly for those who do their alchemy at home; making the silver elixir outside of a laboratory can cause the silver tonic to be ineffective.

Silver has been proven to kill or destroy many different microbes, but one U.S. politician believed it could cure the threat of the Y2k bug when he began taking silver in 1999. We now know nothing happened when the ball dropped at the beginning of the new millennium, but the perceived shortage of antibiotics caused by Y2k disruptions caused fear in many.

Stan Jones, a socially conscious politician known for his stance on the death penalty and opposing same sex marriage, has been taking silver as a home remedy for decades. His blue skin quickly became the main talking point in his unsuccessful runs for the U.S. Senate and governor of Montana.

People ask me if it's permanent, and if I'm dead - I tell them I'm practicing for Halloween- Stan Jones.

During his campaigns, media outlets swarmed Stan Jones, inquiring about his skin more than his policies and stance on government issues. Although Stan's dreams to become a U.S. senator, seem to be behind him at the age of 74. He currently works as a business consultant in Bozeman, Montana. Oh, and Stan Jones still drinks colloidal silver despite his blue skin.

DID YOU KNOW?

The Moors ruled Spain for 800 years introducing new sciences and alchemy to Europe. The Moors had extensive knowledge of gold's conductive power, and during their reign, it was considered a golden age in Spain and Portugal.

6

THE MANY USEFUL BENEFITS OF GOLD & SILVER

Gold in Electronics

The primary use people associate with gold is in jewelry, but gold's use in the industrial industry, mainly manufacturing electronics, has surged in the last decade. The increase of electronics like cellphones, GPS systems, and televisions require gold within the components to keep voltage and current free of corrosion. Gold is one of the best conductors of electricity man has today.

Almost every switch, relay, connecting wire, and soldered joint involves gold because it has been proven to be highly reliable against tarnish in electronic products. Microprocessors and memory chips in computers contain gold on the end of the connection strips. Most large electronic appliances such as billboard sets also include gold components. Electronic gold production takes up 34% of gold's use in the United States, surprisingly more than coinage demands.

If you own an iPhone or any cell phone for that matter, you're carrying fifty cents to a dollar worth of gold in your pocket. That minute amount of gold may not seem like much. Still, as stated earlier from chapter four on electronic waste, discarded cell phones quickly add up in landfills for a lucrative payday later.

Constant updates of cell phone technology create an average lifespan of under two years for cellphones, with very few being recycled. Large quantities over time produce large amounts of gold ready to be used. Don't be surprised if you start looking around your living room for all the electronics that may carry gold inside the battery inserts.

Gold in Dentistry

Got a toothache? Well, man has found a solution for this common ailment 3,000 thousand years ago and has been using gold to fill cavities and rotten teeth ever since. According to the *American Dental Association,* the first book in America published on dentistry by Richard Skinner in 1801 was intended for the common public to grasp fundamental issues with teeth. "Among the services he offered was tooth transplanting, setting human teeth on silver and gold, fixing artificial teeth, filling cavities, teeth extraction, and eradicating tartar and teeth cleaning."

Robert Freeman, the first African American dentist in America, mentored and aided in setting gold in the teeth of ex-slaves and black youth interested in pursuing dentistry. *George Washington,* who was America's first president, had false teeth. Rumors began floating around. They were made of wood, but any sensible person would know getting a splinter in your gums would be very painful. His dentures were poorly made from various items, gold being one of them but never wood, contrary to popular belief.

The Hip-Hop community revolutionized gold teeth in the southern states with the explosive popularity of permanent gold grills. Gold teeth have been used since the days of ancient Kemet; in modern times, dentists are still using gold for fillings, crowns, bridges, and orthodontic appliances.

Medical Uses of Silver & Gold

Who would think silver and gold could help with your grandmother's achy joints, rid people of the common cold or treat burn victims. Those who are aware of this newfound use, silver and gold, will come back in conventional medicine. Gold's dentistry advances quickly switched over to medicine once doctors realized gold fillings stopped decay in teeth and inflammation on the gums. Another form of inflammation in the joints that plagues millions of people called arthritis can be eased when a type of gold sodium solution is injected into the problem area.

Silver in the late 1800s has been proven by German eye doctor *Dr. K.S.* F. Crede to prevent and kill any secondary infection of the eye right after the birth of newborn babies. Thanks to his medical practices, the law in the United States, Canada, and Denmark required these silver nitrate eye drops. Considered the best natural germ fighter in the world, silver kills even the most stubborn pathogens that have grown resistant to antibiotics.

Surgeons rely on silver-laced bandages and other medical accessories that fight infection, which is the most significant danger after a surgical procedure. According to *Health Newsline,* silver is used in many burn centers in the U.S., and UCLA medical labs found it effective against every virus they tested it on. Although not tested or approved by the F.D.A., many believe colloid gold drinks may help strengthen nerve function. Medical uses of gold have expanded dramatically, although still too costly, have shown excellent results.

Today's surgeons use gold to patch and repair blood vessels, nerves, teeth, and even bones. More frequently, surgeons are picking up gold instruments to clear the patient's coronary arteries and tumors. If your silver jewelry turns blue when worn for too long, it could be an indication the wearer has elevated sodium levels in their blood. So just a reminder, when you see a silver ring or necklace turn blue, you now can give someone or yourself a diagnosis to change their diet and cut back on salty snacks.

FUTURE USES OF GOLD

Gold's use in space is not as far in the future as you think because it is already happening. Agencies like NASA spend billions of dollars on satellites. A lack of accessibility in the vastness of space makes maintenance and repair impossible, so building heat shields out of a dependable metal like gold amongst other parts is essential for satellites and other equipment. This is precisely why gold is used in numerous ways in every space vehicle that NASA launches for future space travel.

NASA is already on-board as it launched a $1 billion asteroid study and sample-return mission in 2016. The plan is to explore the Bennu asteroid, which is about 1,614 feet in diameter, with the OSIRIS-REx probe and returns to Earth with a sample in 2023.

Mining for gold in space may be the next gold rush of the future. An article in the *New York Post* explains the possible lucrative business of mining asteroids that fly by Earth's orbit. "There are three types of asteroids: "C-type," "S-type," and "M-Type."

S-types contain high concentrations of metal, iron, nickel, and cobalt but little water, while M-types are the most lucrative, boasting ten times the amount of metal. C-type asteroids the most common type, making up seventy-five percent of asteroids contain hydrated clay materials that can be mined for water in space.

This water could then be turned into rocket propellant via a process called electrolysis, which might one day allow astronauts to refuel their crafts in space and explore even deeper into the cosmos."

The cosmic leftover from these asteroids also contains gold and an essential element of all frozen water. Multiple corporations and mining companies will capitalize on the iron, nickel, carbon, cobalt, and other precious metals on these space rocks. It's no secret these precious metals are slowly being depleted on Earth or in limited supply, and it is only natural for man to look toward the cosmos for new riches in the future.

7
HIP-HOP'S LONG INFATUATION WITH BLING!

Rappers of the present have to come fully loaded when showing off their wealth. Whether it is charting the Billboard Top 100, remaining certified in the streets, or purchasing thousands of dollars in custom jewelry, there is no half-stepping when claiming the title of most dapper in hip-hop culture. Gold jewelry is mistaken as tacky to those foreign to the hip-hop culture, a waste of wealth, and a show of flashy luxurious living. Those that do understand hip-hop culture realize its purpose as a triumph trophy to the impoverished. Its real meaning is the symbolism that reaches back to African royalty if you do the knowledge.

Its current meaning is increasingly being exploited as time goes on by mumble rappers with a penchant for diamond chains. The intention of jewelry in hip-hop is only beneficial to enhance what was already there, yet so many use it to improve what isn't. In the 80s, 90's and early 2000's only individuals with courage, neighborhood respect, and distinction could wear these ornaments of jewelry until hip-hop began utilizing the mainstream hype from the street into their most expensive items of eminence.

The golden era of hip-hop ushered in truck jewelry, a large and in charge style from the 1980s that included fat gold chains, aka dookie ropes, and four-finger rings. Historically, music was written and performed to fit specific social occasions until Hip-Hop hit the scene where so-called street people picked up an instrument called a microphone. Remember the visually hypnotizing bling-bling era of rap in the late 1990s and mid-2000's. Street flashy hip-hop acts like the Cash Money Millionaires, Lil Kim, Master P, Jay-Z, and Diddy drinking expensive champagne waving diamond-encrusted Rolex watches out of European luxury vehicles music videos. Well, today's hottest rap superstars like Lil Yatchy and Meek Mill still adorn themselves in triple gold Cuban link chains and heavy pendants. Why, you ask? These gold, platinum, and diamond items of extravagancc were deemed as trophies or rewards from the struggle of ghetto living, showcasing those artists newfound gold and multi-platinum record sales status to the world, for those in the Hip-Hop community interested in what type of chain or bracelet to buy at the jewelry store. A sure bet is the Miami Cuban link, this type of jewelry uses a lot of gold and is hand-made, which gives it an incredible resale value compared to other kinds of jewelry.

GRAMS & GOLD CHAINS

In the late 1970s through the mid-1980s, change was everywhere in American society; there were anti-drug commercials, the ending of the Vietnam war, environmental movements, and an ongoing economic recession. Disco was dying, and the Bronx was burning building by building as a new generation began to emerge from the underbelly of the slums. The South Bronx was left numb from the destructive effects of a new drug called crack, an addictive hardened form of cocaine.

Crack offered a short but intense high to smokers, and the drug hit every major inner city in America with devastating rates of violence and crime. How does this tie in with gold's influence in Hip-Hop today, you ask? Well, a lot actually; the first Hip-Hop stars dressed much like their disco predecessors until crack cocaine became profitable on the inner-city streets. Once the gritty streets intertwined with hip-hop, its fashion pioneers brought new brands and expensive jewelry to the game from the massive amounts of money they earned.

It adapted the designer labels and melodically punchy dialogue from Blaxploitation films like Dolemite and tracksuits inspired by B-Boys. Hip-Hop was the new wild style, presumably; whatever Hip-

Hop culture touched, it made it more refreshing. This culture of violence, drugs, and extravagance may be cliché to Hip-Hop, but it did not start that way.

By the late 80's inner-city dealers quickly became millionaires off the grams of crack they sold in the streets. Gold chains provided an instant visual cue of wealth and gave a clear message of status without saying a word. Gold jewelry made people feel important. This also intensified the dealing drug lifestyle to disenfranchised impressionable youth, making pawn shops and jewelry shops profit immensely. Hip-Hop culture is now addicted to grams of cocaine and gold chains that cemented into the culture with gangster rap.

Hip-Hop's Love for Karats & Clarity

Hip-hop, in its infancy, followed a set of elements that would allow everyone that was down to partake but your reputation and dedication had to be based on what you did on the streets. Those five elements being Dee-Jaying, Microphone Checking, Breakdancing, Graffiti, and Knowledge.

A breeding ground for rawness, attitude, and creativity, the hip-hop founders may have forgotten one more element in Hip-Hop, which would have to be the conspicuous consumption of getting fly. In certain main-stream, hip-hop circles showcasing wealth to its highest degree is the status quo. Movies and television shows *like Super-Fly, Scarface, Miami Vice, Lifestyles of the Rich and Famous,* and *MTV cribs* attributed to force-feeding distinct values into hip-hop culture.

Those values meant that to be accepted into society, one had to be flashy, successful, and get rich or die trying. [1]Hip-Hop artist that wanted early recognition began dressing like the 5% nation or Poor Righteous Teachers, local street crews like Paid in Full Posse, Lo-Life's and drug lords from their neighborhoods, so it was only natural that gold jewelry was essential to their notoriety and one of the steps to becoming a star in the inner city.

I believe in the future Hip-Hop scholars will study how quickly and effectively a culture created by African Americans looking to express themselves through music changed the precious metal business forever. Any rap artist striving to reach the ranks of the wealthy tax bracket through an art-form based on the underdog and achieves success is praised.

That achievement is honored and flaunted by a demographic of people that can relate. High-end jewelry's connection with Hip-Hop symbolizes and will continue to express escaping the struggle as Hip-Hop evolves and creates a new breed of M.C. I am sure denoting your status through jewelry will be here to stay. Wearing jewelry or some type of ornamentation by making do with what is available to you is what Hip-Hop is all about.

THE SKI MASK WAY; WHO THE HECK IS THE STICKUP KID 50 CENT?

This new Hip-Hop environment of fast profits and flashy jewels brought notorious stick-up kids that had a dangerous penchant for acquiring gold jewelry by any means to the forefront. In rap's storied history, these individuals emerged in its earliest days but rarely highlighted in the culture mainly out of fear, anger, or embarrassment of losing a gold chain.

Street crews birthed in the housing projects like the A-Team, Lo-Life's, Supreme Team, 41 Crew, and Paid in Full Posse, among many others, earned respect by wearing the most dipped out gold jewelry and having the most money.

They were obtaining legendary names like King Tut, Killer Ben, the Terrible Timmons twins, Sticky Fingaz, and the famous K-Sun, just to name a few of the stick-up artists that brought fear and terror throughout the five boroughs. The influx of robbing drug dealers and snatching gold chains at skating rings and subway stations became commonplace. "50 Cent" soon put together his troop of treacherous young guns.

They preyed on pizza deliverymen, hapless storekeepers, and intoxicated club patrons who forget to tuck in their gold in public. They collected a generous pile of cash from jacking designer purses and snatching chains at the Roxy disco in Manhattan, Empire Skating Rink, and Albee Square Mall in Brooklyn."

Kelvin Martin, aka the original 50 Cent, grew up as friends with Eric B. in Brooklyn and was feared by many on New York City streets for his brash muggings. Known to have a small statue of only five feet, two inches, 50 Cent carried two guns, a Colt .45 and .357 Magnum, and did not hesitate to use them to relieve victims of their valuables and jewelry.

Most people have no idea how he acquired the nickname well before rapper Curtis Jackson aka 50 Cent, used it as a pen name to rap stardom and street credibility. Some say Kelvin Martin was given the unusual nickname 50 due to his reputation of being prepared to rob anyone at any time, including rap celebrities, even if they only had 50 cents in their pocket. No matter how much money or gold people were carrying, 50 Cent was willing and prepared to take it.

Stickup kid 50 Cent spent his stolen earnings on European vehicles and lots of gold jewelry, but his materialism quickly turned his friends into victims tarnishing his name on the streets. Now deceased at the tender age of twenty-three, the repercussions of living the life of an outlaw, Kelvin Martin, aka the original 50 Cent, brought in the manifesto how to rob Hip-Hop of its luxury and birthed the chain snatcher mentality.

50 Cent allegedly robbed the likes of LL Cool J, various fats cats, pimps, drug dealers, and maimed dozens of others during his Billy the Kid antics of the Ronald Reagan era. Wearing jewelry with confidence in the Hip-Hop culture during the insurgence of the stick-up kid showed wealth and respect and a fearless attitude towards the many dangers wearing gold attracted in the inner city.

DID YOU KNOW?

Bernhard Goetz, a New Yorker fed up with being a victim of several stickups and robberies in 1984. Shot four African American teens that sparked a nationwide debate on race and crime in major U.S. cities. Goetz was robbed of his watch, wallet, and other valuables before arming himself as he commuted to work. Stickup men plagued the New York City subway systems during the 1980s, with the Goetz case becoming one of the boiling points.

Eric B. and Rakim took the teachings of the 5% nation and the term golden era hip-hop to a whole new level. Even in the present day, few rappers have amassed or surpassed their love for gold. The amount of gold worn by each individual in the 1980s, if valued today, would be worth $100,000 per person, and yes, you heard that correctly $100,000 each.[1]

BLING-BLING TO CORPORATE THUGGING: 2000-PRESENT

Rap in the present is now a multi-billion-dollar industry that has seen its ups and downs as a genre. The jewelry in Hip-Hop appears to get bigger, flashier, and more creativity into the new millennium. Magazines such as *The Source, Vibe Magazine,* and *XXL* highlighted page after page of hip hop's kings of bling.

The stakes on spending were higher, and the diamonds nothing less than VVS. By the mid-2000s, corporate America backed artists like Nelly, 50 Cent, and Jay-Z with sponsorship royalties and liquor deals worth millions of dollars. Southern rap moguls made riches off bling raps covered their smiles with grills made with high-quality diamonds. Mike Jones, the telephone number reciting rapper from Houston, Texas, achieved double platinum record sales for his album *Who Is Mike Jones?* He spent a whopping one million dollars on his hundred karat Ice Age pendant showing and proving he was Houston's very own Iceman.1

Rap artists like Lil Wayne spent hundreds of thousands of dollars on his new set of grills, but his mentor's brothers Bryan *"Birdman"* and Ronald *"Slim"* Williams would take hip-hop jewelry to heights that exceed imagination. Everything had to evoke the illustrious high life helicopters, Lamborghini's, and big money, precisely what Cash Money Records represented.

Every member of the Hot Boys wore a $20,000-dollar diamond pendant that advertised the label's brand. The *"Checkmate"* album by rapper B.G. in 2000 oozed opulence as the rapper wore not one but four Rolex watches, two on each wrist, to be exact. Even if you've never been to New Orleans, Cash Money Records highlighted the south's coming from nothing into something persona to the fullest. Expensive cars, gold grills, and wads of cash mixed in with street tales, a second line bounce, and dope dealing had the world all ears.

The Hip-Hop world has seen veterans' entrepreneurship ability in the game like Jay-Z, Master P, J-Prince, and Russell Simmons go global. Like most radical moguls in the Hip-hop genre, they share a similar story that involves living in the inner city streets to landing record deals and building their labels from the ground up with tremendous success. The newest examples of rap entrepreneurs such as the late Nipsey Hussle or Rick Ross can still be found wearing large amounts of gold jewelry at their concerts and rap videos but took the corporate model to a whole new level. Nipsey Hussle is the most remarkable example of this motto with his reproach of limited creative control and artist's music ownership.

On his Grammy-nominated rap album "Victory Lap" he spits words of a real gold investor in the song by the same name. *"Every few shows I buy some new gold circle got smaller; everybody can't go. Downtown diamond district, jewelers like "Yo, Hussle holler at me, I got Cubans on the low"* Yes, rap audiences have heard lyrics stating the prominence of an artist's jewelry but never to this level of honesty and investment know-how. Hussle shows the factual aspects of his record label all money in no money out, even when purchasing something considered a liability such as gold jewelry.

Whether it's his multiple side hustles, including the Marathon Clothing Store, Cryptocurrency, Elite Human Hair, or Vector 90, a co-work space includes a STEM program that allows inner-city youth from the Los Angeles area the training ability to work in Silicon Valley. Nipsey Hussle was determined to bring the Hip-Hop business from the gritty streets to the owning of his masters in the corporate boardroom.

Instead of sporting a three-piece suit, he could be found wearing five 250-gram gold Cuban link chains with a gaudy Malcolm X pendant. Due to this, he will forever be forged among the great M.C.s and hustlers for his business acumen. Although Ermias Asghedom, aka Nipsey Hussle's life, ended at the age of 33, his impact is stamped on the minds of entrepreneurs worldwide. That blueprint set in stone and the marathon will continue for future Hip-Hop generations that will now understand splurging on expensive jewelry is cool but reinvesting and taking pride in ownership is even cooler.

8

IMPORTANT REASONS TO OWN INVESTMENT GOLD

When talking about investing in precious metals, most of the populous are profoundly confused about what real wealth is. Some people would say gold is not worth its investment potential outside of jewelry, and its softness makes it useless to do much with industrially.

In this book's previous chapters, I explained how gold was valued much differently in today's complex economic environment than during ancient times. Many new investment options have shown up on the market, for example, cryptocurrency, pushing gold investment lower on the priority list, especially with investors from the younger generations.

I'm not telling you not to invest in cryptocurrency, but I am also saying I do not believe it will fix all your investment or financial problems. Economist *Mark Skousen* said it best, explaining his view on Bitcoin, also known as digital gold replacing the insurance of owning actual gold. "Bitcoin is not an actual physical coin, and if computers shut down, you can't buy or sell them. I believe gold and Bitcoin will represent one in the same in the future. Gold will be the old version of wealth storage and Bitcoin the new. Both will always hold value intrinsically.

Like Mr. Skousen, I believe it is imperative to own investments to secure your assets from any hard-economic times that may arise in the future. Gold is money, and by cash, I mean gold is an actual store of value that holds its purchasing power over time. Ask the average person on the street the difference between money and currency I'm willing to bet most will get it wrong on the correct definition.

The first mistake to avoid when investing in precious metals is understanding that currency is not money; it is solely a medium of exchange used to purchase something with liquid or asset value. Currency holds no real value; it is just a middle man of sorts to exchange goods or services for something of actual value.

This means currency can be anything seashells, beads, or whatever society creates value to mimic's actual purchasing power. On the other hand, money has real value within itself, such as gold and silver, or what the finance circles call hard commodities. Paper currency or *fiat* currency is considered a currency but only sometimes considered money if only if a physical silver or gold standard back it.

It doesn't sound obvious, huh? Most people do not understand the difference between the two by design. These two terms are fundamental in economics but are used loosely in society and never taught in our school system. The United States constitution has written in law that only gold and silver are money. Still, the federal reserve has given the populous fiat currency, which over time creates a debt-based monetary system the founding fathers discouraged. What provides a dollar bill value is the United States government's backing stating the currency is a means of exchange for any amount worth of gold or silver stored in the Fort Knox reserve.

Millions of Americans believe the $20 or $50-dollar bill in their pocket stamped as a federal reserve paper note is actually worth $50 or $20, but it is not. It is *fiat* meaning currency thats backed by nothing except government promises. The word *fiat* is a latin word described as money that is circulated by force. If people have confidence in *fiat* money and there is enough government force to push that currency it continues to be used until people lose confidence in that currency. When you own gold to invest in, you will quickly learn the price of gold fluctuates with the rising and falling of the economic market. Gold is essential because it keeps economies in check and rises during uncertain times; almost all the world's currencies are *fiat*.

Anyone with common sense knows promises get broken all the time, and a rise in the price of gold like we saw in the years 1980, 2008, and 2011 is a red flag that the value of government currency and economic conditions are weakening. The source of this is a breeding ground for currency debasement, financial crisis, and ultimately recessions due to the federal reserve printing more paper money to stimulate a weak debt-ridden economy, thus inflating the dollar and manipulating the price of gold.

In the worst-case scenario, the market can control the price of gold for a while with interest rate adjustments. But eventually, as the debt and deficit continue to soar, the physical demand will exhaust supply, possibly crashing the dollar. People will panic or realize that cashing in their gold ETFs or taking physical possession of their money is no longer an available option from the banks. In a panic, our government will have to pay off our enormous debt by creating more *fiat* currency.

The United States dollar bill at some point will have no purchasing power, all fiat currencies have gone to zero and the dollar will be no different but will always accept physical gold and silver. For those that like to remain more on the optimistic side of things, let's say the dollar's purchasing power continues strong in the future. You can liquidate and use all the silver and gold saved over the years for retirement or as a form of nonperishable savings. There is always going to be a risk when investing in anything especially precious metals.

Still, it's fair to say owning investment bullion outside of the banks where you can lay your hands on it has always been the ultimate store of value, and it is the perfect hedge against inflation, crashed economies, and currency debasement. The economy fluctuates in cycles, and it's best to prepare with a sound investment for those dips in the sequence.

STORING YOUR GOLD IN THE BANK?

Many people may be encouraged to store their gold and silver in the bank for safekeeping instead of holding it on their person or in their homes for good reason. Gold is expensive and can quickly become an invitation for thieves once compiled in large amounts. Obviously, they are ways to combat that, such as utilizing heavy-duty safes and keeping your mouth shut to people you do not trust what you own and do not own in regards to precious metals.

Yet, most people that invest heavily in gold or silver quickly realize storage may become limited, or trusting in the security of a banking institution appears more secure than anything they could provide by their own means.

Gold storage is not like storing paper currency in the bank; in fact, it's much more complicated than that. It turns out; your bank has no legal or fiduciary obligation to give you back either your money or your gold if they deem it to be in their best interest not to do so. For example, during a financial meltdown like a depression or a World War, especially if the bank itself has to desperately pay down their own lingering bad debt.

When the bank closes its doors, your money and gold will be gone with it. This isn't meant to scare people but to inform them to keep tabs on deposit boxes. Appreciating gold has been made difficult solely because we live in a heavily cash-based society since the 1970's when we got off the gold standard. People do not understand gold's potential or doubt it is actually something of value in the event of an emergency. When you tune into or read about the stock market, gold isn't something that is brought up unless times are hard and hoarding takes hold.

Keeping your gold is even harder because it is something that is sought after by everyone regardless of class or social background. Driving through any major city, you are bound to see signs stating, "We buy gold" or countless pawn shops that allow people to trade precious metals for paper money. If you do not have to, do not sell your gold because there is an old saying used by investors called "If you don't hold it, you don't own it," and it is something people should remember when tempted to sell or trade-in gold.

DID YOU KNOW?

Gold jewelry has even found its way into the football arena. In 2017, the University of Miami began rewarding its football players with the infamous "turnover chain" after forcing an interception or landing a touchdown. The chain is a 36-inch, 2.5-kilogram, 10-karat gold behemoth of jewelry with a 6.5-inch-wide "U" from the school's logo as the pendant.

ADDITIONAL ECONOMIC DEFINITIONS

Inflation: A general increase in prices and fall in the purchasing value of money.

Deflation: Reduction of the general level of prices in an economy.

Fiat currency: A currency that a government has declared to be legal tender, but it is not backed by a physical commodity.

Money: A medium of exchange that settles payments.

Currency: A generally accepted form of money such as gold or silver.

Bullion: Gold, silver, or other precious metals in the form of bars or ingots. Typically, bullion is used for trade on the market.

HOW FORT KNOX GOT ITS GOLD & WHY ITS KEPT THERE

Completed in 1936 during the Great Depression, the highly secure Fort Knox building was utilized to hold some of the United States' large gold deposits. In conjunction with the Gold Reserve Act of 1934, Fort Knox was created to meet storage demand. President Roosevelt outlawed all bullion ownership and forced all U.S. citizens to sell it, causing the treasury department's vaults to fill up with gold quickly.[1]

Many theories and conspiracies have arisen to the whereabouts and origins of Fort Knox's gold, and by the 1970s, finance attorney Peter David Beter claimed an idea the gold was sold off to shadow governments and world leaders. In 1974, one hundred and twenty reporters and members of Congress were allowed inside to refute the claims of Peter Beter, which were proven to be untrue. The American public observed all alleged gold in Fort Knox was visible and accounted for on national television.

The term *"As safe as Fort Knox"* continues to be proven correct. Keeping the gold safe are heavily armored security personnel down in four armored guard boxes on each building corner. The vault is drill, torch, and blast-proof, equipped with an escape tunnel and razor wire and minefields, to name a few of the security measures.

Fort Knox is an Army post-built-in 1918, and the bullion depository that houses the gold is built on the Army base grounds. If anyone is asking why gold is kept at this location, there is your answer. Suppose you had a choice to store hundreds of billions of revenue worth of gold anywhere; what better place than an active Army base. No member of the public is allowed in or on Fort Knox grounds, so evidence of the gold's existence in the vaults since 1974 is a mystery.

DID YOU KNOW?

The United States gold and silver bullion is housed between four different secure locations and contrary to popular belief not all is in Fort Knox. The rest of it resides at the U.S. Mint at Denver (1,400 tons) and at West Point (1,700 tons) and in the deep storage vaults of the New York Federal Reserve (400 tons). The gold at Fort Knox is stored in one of the most secure facilities in the world.

THE HUNT BROTHERS

I doubt the saga of one wealthy family who crashed the price of silver in 1980 will reach your economic textbooks any time soon. Most people know little about the Hunt family or their greed for silver. In the 1970s, the Hunt brothers decided to shake up the banking world by cornering the silver market. During Jimmy Carter's presidency, high inflation amongst other factors tanked the economy, making millions of Americans doubt their financial security, including the Hunts. How they did it, how much they made, and ultimately caused them to lose their massive silver hoard is nothing short of the most extraordinary silver story ever told.

Brothers Nelson and Herbert Hunt, who were already very wealthy from the Hunt family's multiple businesses, including livestock, oil refineries, and real estate, gained interest in silver investing after reading Jerome Smith's best-selling book *Silver Profit's in the '70s*. Due to falling oil prices in Libya, the Hunt Brothers quickly started losings millions in oil inheritance revenues and were hungry to become tycoons of new investment, the silver market. Silver in 1973 was very cheap, somewhere around $1.50 an ounce. Hence, the Hunt brothers capitalized off silvers underappreciated attention and purchased thousands of ounces, shooting the price of silver up to $3 an ounce. The large amount of silver they bought was a sure sign the Hunts were betting big and literally on their way to owning a large chunk of silver in the United States.

You'll also recall that until 1975, it was illegal for U.S. citizens to buy physical gold. So, the Hunt Brothers focused on silver because they believed it would serve as a haven, just like gold, against inflation and a weak U.S. dollar. -Mike Maloney

U.S. citizens could buy silver and gold through commodities trading, and whoever believes that metal can request delivery of the physical metal into their possession at any time. The Hunts were looking to exploit this clause through futures contracts and surpass another wealthy family; they shared a bitter rivalry. Well aware of the threat of government confiscation and the weakening of the dollar, the Hunts demanded physical delivery of their silver. In early 1974, the commodities market started to react to silver in private hands, further pushing the price of silver upward to around $6 an ounce. Once again, in reaction to the price jump, the Hunts, who were very wise investors gathered the silver they owned, loaded it on a plane and flew it to Switzerland to keep safe.

It seemed the Hunt brothers kept a low profile until 1978 before attempting to take another shot at the silver market. One thing that would allow this next attempt was something significant even if you're not as rich as the Hunt's. That thing is credit, which the Hunt's would use to fund purchasing massive amounts of silver. Good credit attracted wealthy speculators willing to invest in the two brothers, mainly those from the newly formed OPEC and Saudi families.

New funding allowed the Hunts to buy more and more silver, but when they were introduced to the wealthy oil Sheiks in 1978, that's when things got crazy. Nelson Hunt, Herbert Hunt and several Saudi princes acting as a discreet front for Sheik Khalid bin Mahfouz. The International Metals Investment Company in Bermuda was created to house silver in case the Sheik was overthrown. This company's sole purpose was to buy silver contracts on credit and then demand delivery of the silver to various off-shore banks.

This silver storage at IMIC would then be a hedge against oil shortages and embargoes for the Sheik and long-term safe preservation of wealth for the Hunt family. This move also caught the United States government's attention looking into Middle Eastern involvement in altering American silver reserves. A media frenzy erupted around the Hunts known to be very private but finally broke the ice to congress and spoke about their opinions on private silver ownership.

The public response pissed of the Federal Reserve Chairman who ordered institutions lending large sums of money to investors that bought precious metals to stop immediately. By 1979 the Hunt brothers owned an estimated 4.5 billion dollars worth of silver on paper. The price of silver was $50 an ounce, but the Hunts kept buying silver. Eventually, what they were asking for could not be met. The silver on the reserve was dangerously low, and the futures trading industry was on edge.

COMEX created the Silver 7 rule in response: the silver bullet that would finally knock down the two brothers' silver spending spree. Taking advantage of their greedy borrowing habits and increasing the margin call requirements. The Hunts could no longer receive credit to buy more silver, trade it on the commodities market, or pay the enormous credit margin bill and silver storage fees, sending silver price into freefall.

Wall Street went into a panic after the brothers received a 100-million-dollar margin call and could not pay the bill or ask the banks for a loan. Now etched in history as *Silver Thursday*, the silver stock fell from $50 an ounce to $11, and the Hunts ran out of money. The aftermath was so chaotic the U.S. government considered a bailout for the Hunts since they had so much of the world's silver tied up in debt, but congress vetoed it.

Nelson and Herbert miraculously received a bailout from private banks and companies. Still at the cost of being fined very heavily and forced into bankruptcy. In the end, it took a decade to sell all the silver they owned plus the selling of other profitable businesses to pay the final bill leaving them billions of dollars poorer. Although they still had enough money to lose on the level they did. It was a spit in the Hunt family's face and a real example of what Alan Greenspan, former Federal Reserve chairman, coined excess irrational exuberance. [1]

2007-2009 FINANCIAL CRISIS

When I wrote this book, the worst of the financial crisis had already ended ten years ago. Ten years is a long time, heck most people cannot remember what they did ten minutes ago, so reliving the financial crisis that sent bankers pleading for a government bailout is distant to most.

In 2007, the economy was in bad shape. By 2008, the housing market nearly crashed, causing millions into foreclosure and loss of employment. On the other hand, gold was still cheap before the crisis going for $635 an ounce in 2006. As gold does in hard times, it becomes more and more valuable as faith in the economy faltered by 2008. That same bar of gold by 2009 cost $1,087.

Understanding what caused this massive surge in the gold price, we have to precisely examine what triggered the financial crisis and its role in it. As we now know, the Bear Stearns bailout caused by failed subprime mortgage lending, and the recession sent shock waves through the gold market as investors panicked to pick up the pieces.

They were panicking for a good reason. Bear Stearns was an investment bank with 85 years of banking experience, survived the 1929 Wall Street crash, and held $350 billion in assets. The bailout ultimately was not enough to save the company, and went it defunct almost overnight.

The closure caused a ripple effect through the stock market as several central investment banks collapsed like dominoes. According to *USA Today*, from 2007 to 2012, more than 450 banks failed across the country.

Banks giving bad loans and failing derivatives seemed to be the reoccurring theme to the crisis, but gold began to rally up its worth to patch up the deflating housing bubble. Big investors eager to save their financial future purchased gold in large amounts shooting the price to record highs.

Robert Kiyosaki, the author of *Rich Dad Poor Dad: What the Rich Teach Their Kids*, quoted his investment wherewithal *"A brilliant guy and a sound investor who knows how to connect the dots"* explains one reason for this silent gold rush. "Smart investors know that the stock and bond market have reached their peaks and have been declining for a while now. Those that are financially intelligent and in the know have been quietly moving their money into tangible assets, especially gold and silver."

During the great recession, gold changed the way many investors looked at the money, and the more they bought, the more scarcity of gold increased, sky rocking the price over $1000 an ounce. That gold price was unheard of; even during the Great Depression, gold didn't sell on the market for such high prices. *The Bureau of Labor Statistics* released some staggering figures that reveal gold's runaway price and increase in value. "From September 2010 to September 2011, gold prices jumped 50.6 percent, mainly the result of speculation surrounding an uneven recovery and volatility in the U.S. financial markets, with gold reaching an all-time high of $1,917.90 per ounce in August 2011.

In 2012, price increases for gold slowed, rising less than they had in each of the four previous years. The 5.4-percent increase in 2012 was the smallest yearly gain since the 2.6-percent advance in 2008."

Years after the recession, gold's importance remains high and on everyone's radar as an investment. Companies offering cash in exchange for gold jewelry seemed to pop up everywhere. This major blow to the United States economy allowed other countries to catch up on their gold consumption.

Buying gold has increased since the recession as well but not for Americans, but for countries like China and the Middle East. CEO of *Harry Winston,* Robert Gannicott, explains to *Forbes,* who the most prominent gold buyers are, "Looking forward, we continue to see strong global jewelry and timepiece demand from China while Japan and the Middle East improve and the U.S. remains subdued. On this basis, we expect to continue to grow our jewelry and timepiece business despite challenging economic conditions in the U.S. and Europe.

DID YOU KNOW?

Gold is a popular choice when it comes to rewarding achievement with medals, statues and trophies. Academy Award, Olympic and Nobel Prize winners all receive golden items in recognition of their achievement.

THE FED, GDP & CHINA'S GOLD APPETITE

The U.S. Congress created the FED (Federal Reserve System) in 1913. It is headed by the Board of Governors of the Federal Reserve, who implement monetary policy. The FED acts as the banker for the central government and serves as the bank's banker. The FED acts much like a central bank does in a foreign country but was created by Congress to support the economy's financial system in the United States and its territories abroad.

Real GDP or Gross Domestic Product can be defined as the measure of services or goods valued and produced by an economy in a given year. The GDP price gauges the value and is an early indicator of inflation or deflation of an economy. Deflation occurs when the economic growth is larger than the money the economy can generate.

Inflation is the increase of currency being printed while there is a decrease in economic growth to back up the currency's purpose. Inflation was and continues to be a growing problem for the economy, causing the Federal Government to add steps in 1979 to keep it under control.

When inflation remains high, it causes the dollar's value to decrease, which means the buying power of the dollar drops dramatically, giving the consumer less bang for their buck. Inflation is the increase of currency being printed while there is a decrease in economic growth to back up the currency's purpose. Inflation was and continues to be a growing problem for the economy, causing the Federal Government to add steps in 1979 to keep it under control.

China is the second-largest economy in the world behind the United States and has made clear intentions it wants to control the physical gold market. So, monitoring the U.S. GDP and inflated dollar naturally would revive their appetite for gold holdings.

Let's make one thing clear although the United States has endured a financial crisis and political upheaval; it still ranks number one in terms of the world economy. How long can the United States keep up with China's prospering GDP is up for debate? The amount of gold the United States owns for a good reason is kept a secret, making it almost impossible for competitive countries to be informed.

Chinese banks invite customers to buy gold, sell gold, and use gold as collateral for loans. Government-sponsored advertising plays across China, encouraging citizens to buy and hold gold and silver. News programs update gold and silver prices and alert listeners to bargains in premiums. -Money Metals Exchange

According to Guy Christopher from *Money Metals Exchange,* China fed its gold urges in secret, mainly after the ban on gold ownership was lifted in 2003. "The last official notice of China's gold holdings astounded the financial world. In April 2009, China announced it held 1,054 tons, almost double what was previously known. That lifted China into fifth place among nations holding gold.

That headline helped boost gold prices in the aftermath of the financial crisis of 2008." Ironically, China invented paper money thousands of years ago, but its current economic boom has slowly lost trust in its purchasing power.

The purchase of gold is highly encouraged in Chinese society, but the threat of China becoming number one is also its collective goal of the Chinese state's financial betterment, unlike the division American society is currently experiencing.

Whether undervaluing to fix exports in the 1990s to buying gold in huge imports, each move is flat out strengthening China's position every year. China is a superpower for manufacturing; the *"Made in China"* imprint is a fixture on almost every product, hence Donald Trump's controversial tariff policy.

We pay for those products in GDP China then turns and reinvests into technology or gold investments. According to Gary Shapiro, CEO of the *Consumer Technology Association* told *Fox News*, it's time for Americans to shift gears towards gold investment, the economy, and China's imminent rise. "Even the most casual visitor to China cannot help but see a nation leaping into the future. Thousands of new buildings, roads, and bridges; dozens of new airports; and several maglev high-speed trains – all of it reflects strategic infrastructure investment.

A few years ago, the nation produced copycat technology products, but now it's producing unique, innovative products that its urban population purchases via smartphones. "In the next 15 to 20 years, we may see a new superpower in the global economy, with the United States running second to China or India unless drastic government spending changes are resolved. I have no idea what the future holds for China, The U.S., or other countries' gold reserves.

One thing that is a sure bet, for now, America has stepped back into isolationism instead of pursuing global economic influence like China, and it could very well cause a shift in global gold holdings.

DID YOU KNOW?

On a quarterly basis, China's private jewelry and investment gold demand historically peaks in the January to March period, when the Lunar New Year holidays and gift-giving celebrations spur the heaviest household buying.

9
PRECIOUS METAL INVESTMENT PURCHASING & SELLING FAQ

Both gold and silver can be used to diversify your assets and as an alternative investment in an IRA eligible portfolio. Investment-grade gold and silver have stood the test of time and will continue to do so with real inherent value, so the demand to buy it will remain high. Purchasing investment-grade gold and silver at the market value or spot price is the basis for all pricing per ounce. The premium price is added to the spot price, which finalizes what you pay at the final checkout. If the spot price equals A and the premium price equals B, the final price would be A + B = C.

Investment groups, individuals, and banks actively buy these investment-grade metals as a safe guard. As an investment, silver is used similarly to gold as a hedge against paper currencies' devaluation. Some people like to collect silver and gold, but most invest in it as a rainy day fund if they have to use it to buy goods.

GOLD BULLION

Bullion in gold or silver can be a lucrative way to invest and come in bars and coins. Gold bullion has a very high purity grade of gold somewhere in the 91.8% to 99% range, to be exact, and holds its numismatic value longer than lower karats. This type of gold is generally purchased in the form of coins and is strictly for investment.

The benefit of owning gold bullion is its extreme popularity and availability to be easily purchased in various weights anywhere from half grams to kilos, making it very recognizable to buyers worldwide. Most of the popular forms of gold bullion coins are American Gold Eagles, Gold American Buffalos, South African Krugerrands, Canadian Gold Maple Leaf, and Gold Austrian Philharmonics.

Other popular gold bullions in bars are Pamp Suisse, Credit Suisse, Johnson Matthey, Perth Mint, Valcambi, and Engelhard. Gold bullion can be purchased at any local coin dealer in your area or on reputable websites like Apmex.com, JMBullion.com, and GoldSilver.com in the form of coins, bullion bars, or investment-grade jewelry.

Numismatic Coins

A numismatic coin is a fancy word for a current collector coin. Most numismatic coins minted worldwide are made from gold, generally as a high purity alloy with small amounts of other metals to increase hardness like copper. The price of these coins will be based on three key things metal content, numismatic premium, and dealer profit when attempting to recoup your investment for what you paid for them.

This may not be the best option for the average investor since minor grading differences may make hundreds or even thousands of difference in profit. Numismatic coins can be valuable, and this value can bring dishonest dealers, cons, and phone scammers looking to sell or buy numismatic coins. Once again, investing in collector coins requires knowledge and experience, so you may want to choose different investing options if you are a novice.

EXCHANGE TRADED FUNDS & FUTURES

People who find it inconvenient or unsafe to physically possess gold or silver can trade it on the stock market if they want to diversify their wealth. Exchange-traded funds, better known as ETFs, are a great option. Like a stock, ETF's track the price of gold, allowing the investor a different option for those that still want to invest in gold.

In 2011, gold skyrocketed over two thousand dollars per ounce, making investing in ETFs very worthwhile. Exchange-traded funds invest the money collected from the purchase of gold bullion traded on the stock exchange.

There are many investment options out there, such as silver futures. Futures are contracts that the purchaser agrees to buy X amount of precious metals on the day of the futures contract due date. Due to a significant chance, the silver price will change between the time you buy the silver and the time you take delivery.

It is not recommended to invest in futures for the long term silver stacker. Most futures require a minimum buy-in amount before a contract can be finalized, somewhere around four or five thousand ounces. The issue is that you pay for your silver at the time of purchase, not the delivery. If the delivery is several weeks or months later, there's a chance that the price of silver may drop or rise.

The silver seller would make a very nice profit and the buyer a big loss depending on the moment in the market because they do not have to retrieve the metal until it is time to deliver. This vacillation level is enough to scare off most investors or people with limited funds that want to buy into the futures contract. Also, you incur additional fees for shipping and delivering large amounts of silver.

Ultimately, as previously stated, it's not the right way for new investors or those with limited funds to get into precious metals investing. ETFs, the other option mentioned, are mostly pieces of paper or computer-based derivatives attempting to track the silver price with a supposed silver bullion backing that is getting stored outside of the investor's knowledge.

GOLD NUGGETS & BULLION JEWELRY

Protecting your financial future by purchasing natural gold nuggets and bullion jewelry is another popular way to invest in gold discreetly. Unlike traditional gold bullion, gold nuggets also fall into the mineral category adding additional value as a collectible item when purchased as an investment. Gold nuggets in quartz or larger than average size can bring in significant premiums over spot price.

Bullion jewelry is a portable and discreet way to invest and hold gold as heirlooms for future generations, and the choice on the matter comes down to personal choice. There are several important steps to remember when buying gold for investment purposes, especially jewelry. These tips will also shut down the haters that claim jewelry is a dumb investment decision. Going heavy on your gold jewelry increases its value; the more grams your jewelry weighs, the better the investment return will be.

Your jewelry can be used as a tax write off, especially if it advertises your company name or likeness. Go to an expert gemologist and get all your jewelry appraised, which will save you time and effort for insurance purposes. Lastly, getting an insurance claim on your jewelry will come in handy if stolen or lost. The gemologist's appraisal is usually valued higher than the cost of the jewelry, which will allow the owner to double up on their appraised value if it's lost or stolen.

WHAT IS THE GOLD STANDARD? DO WE NEED IT? COULD IT COME BACK?

The gold standard is a monetary system where a fixed quantity of gold is the standard unit of account. The actual use of gold as money began thousands of years ago in Asia Minor possibility in Lydia. But why gold? Why not a diamond, platinum, or a peanut standard. The gold standard was created when humans accepted gold on a widespread scale as a currency, and without a gold standard, there is a huge risk of an economic global dead zone becoming a reality.

Gold of all the major metals is almost impossible to destroy, limited in supply, and easy to store for long periods, making it the standard of tying a currency to a commodity. Although gold holds its value, the gold standard across the globe has slowly been abandoned since the depression of the 1930s. Why did gold fail as a standard, one may ask, and why did we need a gold standard, to begin with.

All countries had a gold standard at one point or another but cannot increase the money in circulation without having more gold reserves to back it, thus keeping inflation and government overspending at bay. Events like the great depression and deflation caused the economy to be stifled. To prevent the citizens from depleting the gold supply in a panic, interest rates and taxes were raised. The domino effect was businesses could not afford to borrow money, so

President Roosevelt allowed inflation to open up the printing press, which pumped money into the economy and lowered the interest rate. Many people, including politicians like Ron Paul, would like to see the gold standard make a come-back in the American economy. Still, the days of a similar economy where the gold standard could flourish are long gone. A conversion back to a place where every dollar is backed by gold is very unlikely because over trillions of dollars have been printed since the standard was converted in 1971, crushing the Bretton Woods Agreement. This was encouraged even further due to Ronald Regan's demand to remove drug lords and cash abundant foreigners from purchasing up the United States gold supply.

DID YOU KNOW?

A gold watch can be a good investment, but like investing in cars, art, and other tangible assets there is no guarantee to automatically make money unless that watch is in high demand and sold to the highest bidder. If you are interested in a watch that will hold its value over time, Rolexes are a potentially good choice of brand to start.

HOW THE GOVERNMENT CAN CONFISCATE YOUR GOLD: UNDERSTANDING THE FACTS & THE TIMELINE OF GOLD IN THE UNITED STATES MONETARY SYSTEM

Benjamin Franklin famously quoted that "In free governments, the rulers are the servants and the people their superiors and sovereigns" A lot has changed since Benjamin Franklin uttered these words, namely since the government has grown superior and are involved in every facet of Americans lives including the monetary system and their finances. In reality, one of the many ways people can empower wealth for themselves against economic crashes and the devalue of paper money when the government makes the rules is physically owning gold and silver.

The 1930s may seem like a very long time ago, but in the world of government policy, it couldn't be any closer than yesterday—even today with the fear of federal budget shutdowns and tax refunds being withheld from hard-working Americans. Gold plays a self-regulating yet stabilizing part in the global economy, and up until recently, governments could only print as much money as their country had in gold, but what happens when the laws change and printing exceeds gold's supply. People that have some knowledge of investing in a hard commodity like gold or silver may have heard the stories of how the United States government, under the threat of fines or imprisonment, relinquished the public's private gold-stock some eighty years ago.

The threat of the government tapping into the stockpiles of precious metal investor's stashes is very real and could happen again with the stroke of a pen. The CEO of *WealthCycles.com*, Mike Maloney, said it best *"The Constitution did not stop the government from taking peoples gold in 1933. If the government chooses to outlaw private gold ownership again, there is, unfortunately, nothing you or I will be able to do about it."* I will explain the timeline of the history of gold owning regulation in America. No one can tell what years ahead may bring, and the laws can change in the future, but here is what has happened in the past.

October 1929- The stock market crash of 1929 was the greatest financial crash in the United States history, causing an upheaval of Federal Reserve policy and gold regulation for American citizens.

May 1933- President Roosevelt, in a desperate attempt to control the damage of the great depression, the American economy was undersigned Executive Order 6102 outlawing the American people the right to hoard gold. All gold coins, gold bullion, and gold certificates privately owned by U.S. citizens were to be delivered to all federal reserve banks in exchange for paper money almost forcibly. The dissolution of the gold standard act via the order states any U.S. citizen that violated the demands of the executive order could face a $10,000 fine or imprisonment up to ten years, or both.

January 1934- The gold reserve act was enacted in 1934 as a follow up to ratify Executive Order 6102. President Roosevelt was restricted in stimulating the economy due to the system still being heavily intertwined with the gold standard. To get around this stumbling block, the fed banned all exporting and convertibility of gold into paper money, allowing complete control of gold coming in and going out of the country. The federal reserve increased gold's fixed price of $20.67 per troy ounce to $35 per troy ounce, tripling their treasury holds in the process.

August 1971- For thirty-seven years, gold's fixed price remained untouched until Richard Nixon, who was up to his neck in a financial crisis, high rates of unemployment and inflation well over 5.84%, made a desperate decision. Richard Nixon canceled the convertibility of the dollar to gold. This was called the Nixon shock, a series of quick economic measures that ended the Bretton Woods International Monetary System and effectively removed the fixed $35 per ounce for gold to the current system of floating exchange rates.

December 1974- President Gerald Ford, by an act of Congress, repealed the limitation on gold ownership and once again allowed the private ownership of gold coins, bars, and certificates. The gold repeal joint resolution went into effect on December 31, 1974.

October 1977- President Jimmy Carter signed The International Economic Powers Act on October 28, 1977, removing any president's authority to regulate gold transactions during a national crisis other than war.

December 1985- On December 17, 1985, fifty-two years after Theodore Roosevelt signed the executive order that changed the relationship of gold between the government and the public. President Ronald Reagan signed into law the U.S. mint's ability to produce gold coins from mined sources domestic to United States soil. The gold bullion coin act produced the first United States gold coin, called the Gold American Eagle, which today is one of the most well-known gold coins in the world.

The question still remains, will confiscation happen again? I am by no means a gold bureau metals advisor or qualified enough to say, but governments have seized gold from its citizens before, and in times of financial turmoil or war, it's even more likely. The weird thing about gold is understanding the value of a metal that is worthless outside the human perspective. Even Warren Buffet said gold has no intrinsic value. Who knows? What's possible in the future, but the best thing to do is prepare and remain knowledgeable about gold as much as you can.

HOW TO INVEST: DIAMONDS? OR GOLD? GUNS? OR BUTTER? WHAT'S BETTER TO BUY?

Diamonds, gold, guns, or butter? If you were given the option of choosing two out of these four items, you thought would have the most value economically, which would they be? By guns, I don't mean firearms, and the butter I'm talking about isn't the stuff you put on your toast in the morning.

I'm talking assets versus liabilities; gold is only produced by the collision of neutron stars or supernovas. Remember, gold came to earth via meteorites, and there is only a finite amount on the planet. Diamonds are made here on Earth through heat and pressure over time. Man can make diamonds but can't make gold. Although diamonds are expensive, they can lose value quickly if not of high quality, color, and karat. However, gold will always hold value.

If anyone is familiar with the 2001 movie *Baby Boy* written by John Singleton, the guns and butter concept is discussed by ex-con Melvin played by Ving Rhames. The movie is based on the concept that African American males, through fatherless homes, racism, mass incarceration, poverty, and lack of responsibility, go through life as baby boys well into adulthood, never learning true economic empowerment.

Jody, played by actor Tyrese Gibson gets a quick lesson in Macroeconomics from Melvin as he schools him on the rules of financially growing up "You got to learn the difference between guns and butter." There are two types of people, people with guns and people with butter. What are the guns? That's the real estate, the stocks, and bonds.

Artwork. Stuff that appreciates with value. What's the butter? Cars, clothes, jewelry, all the bull-crap that don't mean anything after you buy it. That's what it's all about: Guns and butter, baby. "Simply put, the smart choice out of these four items can vary depending on supply and demand. Some people put more value in butter, but over the long term, those people usually always fail financially. Yet, the people that chose gold as an investment over diamonds and guns over butter from an economic standpoint will always see profit over those who don't.

DID YOU KNOW?

Millions of impoverished children and teenagers are enduring harsh child labor in places like the Philippines, Brazil, Africa, India and China mining for dirty gold in above ground and underwater gold mines. Most children as young as eleven do this to aid in the financial support of their families some only making a few dollars a day. It is dangerous work and many suffocate, or are crushed by rocks or drown doing compressor mining underwater.

SELLING YOUR SILVER AND GOLD IN A WITHOUT RULE OF LAW SCENARIO

Many people, during unprecedented times, pandemics, wars, or nuclear fallout, may wonder how they could sell their precious metals safely and the rules to follow when there is no law and order. This is the stuff preppers dream about, but the nightmare can become very real very fast for the unprepared. During a catastrophic event such as an economic collapse, or you find yourself surrounded by a population that no longer has confidence in the monetary system currently in place would be a good reason to begin panicking. Still, there are a few things you can do to protect yourself and your family.

Every person's situation is different when you consider life hitting the fan and getting worse. For some people, being laid off from a job and losing a wage to pay bills may be incentive enough to sell their precious metals, and for some, that may not be the case. Others would barter their skill sets and knowledge first to earn a wage, gain food, obtain medical supplies, etc., in times of uncertainty, only selling their metals for barter as an absolute last resort.

In the event you do have to sell your silver or gold, it is always wise to do so during normalization periods after the worse of things have settled. People stranded on their roofs during hurricanes are not thinking about precious metals or selling them because, amid chaos, normal life is uprooted. People are living weeks and months in an economic depression where reality has set in that there is no work, banks are not open, and jobs are not paying a livable wage where paper money no longer has value precious metals then come into importance.

Once again, these metals are more so a form of retirement or savings to save yourself from inflation, but you have to sell, look for coin shops first in the event. If open and around, Coin shops will give you the best deal on your metals if you need to sell them. The second option would be to look for pawnshops; granted, they deal with more desperate people, so you may not get your precious metals full value in a sticky situation.

Pawnshops and coin shops more than likely will not be open or in operation during hard times, but if they are, those should be the first places to sell. So, being smart about the reality that you could endanger your safety by being callous about selling precious metals with someone in a mad max world. A great rule to follow is never to carry large amounts of valuables on your person without personal protection or a companion to safely monitor the transaction.

You have to gauge what you are looking for and how much metal is worth the swap. Granted, if the person is honest, handing out coins for trade must be accessed with common sense. Giving someone a ten-ounce bar of silver to change a tire versus a one-ounce gold coin for fixing the roof on your house or providing medical service like surgery, for example, quickly puts things into perspective. You have to decide the value and the services or goods you need compared to what you're giving up in the form of silver or gold.

Bartering coins or bars that are easily recognizable such as American Eagles, Canadian Maple leaf, or China Panda's, reduce the chance someone may turn you down with the suspicion the metal is fake due to them never seeing that type of coin or bar before. People may be new to exchanging metals instead of dollars, so bartering half up front and a half after completion is always a good move during times when there is no police presence to save you if someone is dishonest and wants to relinquish you of your silver or gold.

Precious metals will be a major currency in a financial reset, or at least according to what history has shown us during previous economic cycles in the United States. Skills such as carpentry, medical knowledge, construction, plumbing, and other skills could be helpful. So, it is best to get some of both metals and skills to better prepare yourself for worst-case scenarios that could show up in the future.

WEALTH ACCUMULATION VS DOLLAR ACCUMULATION

How do we measure wealth? Americans like most of the world associate their wealth and experience in paper money. You get an hourly wage in dollars, pay for a gallon of gas at the pump in dollars and trade internationally in dollars. We are trained to think if the dollar goes down in value so does your wealth. Some people that invest in gold and silver that experience a price drop in the metals value naturally believe their wealth has dropped but if they do they don't understand gold and silver's avenue to wealth.

We are taught to work towards retirement and put our dollars into savings as it accumulates wealth over time. We are not taught to stack and save gold and silver for the same cause. People either do not subscribe to look into metal stacking or down right hate it, but you must look at economic history to keep a tally on the future of money and wealth accumulation.

The word tally derives from the tally stick which were used to record quantities of either gold, money or debt. The Ishango bone is a tally stick discovered to be over 20,000 years old making it the oldest known mathematical tool. Money and wealth increase or decrease at certain times, so tally sticks were used in Europe to record these timed cycles well before America won its freedom from England but the cycle of tallying continued in America.

An easier way to simplify this way of thinking imagine it is 1933 and your wealthy great grandfather worked hard and accumulated $560 to buy a Ford Deluxe vehicle. He also bought twenty-eight gold liberty coins which he could go out and purchase the same Ford Deluxe if need be. Here is why accumulating the gold coins will allow you to secure true wealth.

Let's say sixty years go by and its now 1993 during this time a few of these money tally cycles has passed and you stumble across grandpa's old gold coins in a box that had been stored away. You decide you need a new vehicle and have your heart set on a 1993 Ford Taurus. Following grandpa's foot-steps you show up to the car dealership with $560 for a down payment and the twenty-eight gold coins you found. In an instant, you find out $560 is not enough to secure a down payment and the monthly car note is $490 but the twenty-eight gold coins after sixty years have increased in value so much you could buy the car in full removing the need for a down payment or a car payment.

The lesson learned here is accumulating gold is always better than stacking up dollars over time which lose purchasing power. Use the dollars you earn and buy gold and silver that is one of the ways to save money even if it takes sixty years to do so. God forbid gold is outlawed again at the very least you can take the gold you accumulated and get whatever equivalent of money is dished out. **(Please see earlier in the chapter on government gold confiscation for clarity.)**

Once the Great Depression hit with full force, countries once again had to abandon the gold standard. When the stock market crashed in 1929, investors began trading in currencies and commodities. As the price of gold rose, people exchanged their dollars for gold. It worsened when banks began failing. People began hoarding gold because they didn't trust any financial institution. -Kimberly Amadeo

During the great depression, millions of people realized keeping gold close was best but by 1933 it was outlawed for American citizens to own. The people with more gold to redeem for dollars from the Federal Reserve had a better chance making it through the depression. A rule of thumb to always follow when looking into capturing wealth is to research what the banks are stockpiling. Sooner or later you'll find out its gold and other assets. Gold is very important and is the only form of honest money. A true precious metals investor should follow suit.

10

GOLD BEGETS WAR

HITLER'S MAD DASH TO SECURE THE ALLIES GOLD

Many people know Adolf Hitler for being the man who forced the world into a war full of atrocities involving up to 85 million people and 30 different countries.1 World War II brought the loss of millions of lives, the fall of the Japanese and Italian empires, the Holocaust, and the beginning of the nuclear age. Another interesting revelation about World War II is the use of gold, or better yet, Nazi gold played in its creation and ultimate destruction. Hitler's mad scramble and interest to acquire all of the gold in Europe put the Allies and Axis powers in a bloody struggle for ultimate control. This gold, once in Hitler's possession, would allow him to control all of continental Europe and return a resurgence of German pride and wealth to the Aryan people, who he deemed a superior race of human beings. Let's go back to the end of WWI, where Germany saw defeat at the hands of France, to see how and why Germany needed as much gold as possible.

The Treaty of Versailles signed in 1919 forced Germany to demilitarize and pay billions in reparations for the loss and damage inflicted on several countries during the war. Making matters worse, the Great Depression crippled Germany's economy, which lacked any rich resources besides coal. All other items had to be imported into the country. "Unemployment climbed to as high as 30 percent. In his inaugural address via radio, Hitler vowed to "achieve the great task of reorganizing our nation's economy" through "a concerted and all-embarking attack against unemployment." Hitler's rants for economic empowerment initially but was not taken seriously by the League of Nations. In four short years, Hitler tapped into the deficit spending to build railroads, housing, and massive transit projects like the autobahn, ultimately thwarting unemployment. Although unemployment was eased, the German currency was essentially worthless due to hyperinflation, making it hard to buy goods for the war effort from its supplier nations.

This is where gold enters into the mix for Hitler, who quickly realized gold would secure German finances and give them unpreceded power in the region. Hitler truly hated gold and what it stood for; little did the European powers realize Hitler would stop at nothing to obtain the gold bullion they possessed. Going against the treaties signed at Versailles, Germany quickly invaded an unprepared Austria, killing thousands of Jews and stealing all of the country's gold. "The infusion of Austria's 90 to 100 metric tons of hard currency gave Hitler the boost he needed to continue his plundering." 4 Now, building a massive well-fed German army with the best weapons and armada became easy. Every country Hitler invaded was crushed under his Blitzkrieg and out-matched by his elite SS soldiers.

Considered one of the greatest heists of gold in history, the Nazis would go onto steal gold from the central banks of Austria, Poland, Belgium, Holland, and the Netherlands. Millions more in silver, platinum, diamonds, artwork, and other assets were stolen as well. Once the element of surprise was up, several European countries became aware of Hitler's scheme and either shipped their gold bullion overseas to Canada and America or hid it from getting into the hands of the German army. No longer able to plunder gold directly from occupied central banks Hitler's plan B to get more gold would become more-scary and down-right evil as World War II played out for several more years.

DID YOU KNOW?

The present whereabouts of Nazi gold that disappeared has been the subject of several books, conspiracy theories, and a failed civil suit.

OPERATION FISH: THE FIGHT TO SAVE BRITAIN'S BULLION

Winston Churchill, the prime minister of the British empire who defended the country in 1939 from a full-on German assault called the leaders of Canada and America to concoct the plans for the world's most significant transfer of wealth in history. Hitler would stop at nothing to control the British Isles, and like many Allie controlled countries, he crushed before, he planned on stripping Britain of its gold reserves which had some of the most considerable quantities in all of Europe.

British citizens were ordered to deposit any gold they possessed to the central banks to save the country's wealth. Not sure of when impending doom would happen British warships were deployed to accompany Allie merchant ships to evacuate thousands of metric tons of British gold. This gold was on its way to Canada's central bank in Ottawa safely out of the hands of Adolf Hitler. Transferring the gold would be risky across the Atlantic Ocean the waters were infested with German U-boat's which stood responsible for sinking hundreds of Allie and civilian ships.

Miraculously, vessels bogged down with heavy gold bars started reaching Canada despite dealing with bad weather. Worth a mind-boggling $30 billion in value as of 2019, the valuable gold including bullion from France and Norway had moved secretly by ship during the operation which was considered a success.

Some of the British gold would also be used to purchase weapons from the Americans, which Winston Churchill requested months earlier but denied unless he paid in gold. Historian James Powell explains how important gold was in the politics of World War II. "To buy weapons and other war material that is sorely needed from the neutral United States, Britain had to pay in gold or U.S. dollars; no credit was permitted under the strict Neutrality Act in effect in the United States at the time.

Named Operation Fish, Churchill's gamble paid off by 1940 he was successfully able to transfer all the gold. The British bullion stored at an undisclosed location resided 30 feet underground guarded around the clock by Royal Canadian Police. It remained there being utilized as Britain's payment for war expenses until the war was over. The most amazing part about the whole operation had to be not one piece of cargo was lost or stolen during the gold transfer. Neither greed or Hitler who had spies, military intelligence and the upper hand on the Allies at the time never got the gold or infiltrated the mission of Operation Fish.

DID YOU KNOW?

German economists never forgot World War II only trusting gold as money when the financial crisis struck in 2008-2009. Germany became the number one European country in gold investing ploughing as much as $8 billion into gold coins, bars and exchange-traded commodities (ETCs) annually.

GADDAFI'S INFAMOUS GOLD GUN

Muammar Al-Gaddafi at one time was the de facto leader of Libya. His strong military background allowed him to seize control of the North African country in 1969 following a long-term dictatorship until he was ousted in 2011 during the Arab spring. Gaddafi shared one quality some dictators seem to have; the love for gold plated guns. Adolf Hitler, Saddam Hussein, and various Mexican cartel leaders have all had gold guns seized from their residences.

In April 2003, shortly after the U.S. military invaded Baghdad and Saddam Hussein went into hiding, an unidentified U.S. serviceman tried to ship home an AK-47, a pistol, and another rifle to Fort Stewart, Georgia. Unfortunately for him, the "souvenirs" or looted items — depending on how you look at it — were intercepted at London's Heathrow Airport. But these weren't ordinary war trophies: all three weapons were plated in gold. -War is Boring

Along with gold guns, Gaddafi also loved to extravagant forms of displaying his wealth and power. He was known to parade around with an all-female security brigade that wore high heels. Most of his residences were laden with gold furniture, expensive vehicles, and even exotic animals. Social media fueled the Arab Spring in Tunisia and Egypt further as the world watched dictators and rulers that remained in office for decades removed for their injustices and war crimes. The Libyan people, after four decades of Gaddafi's rule, became fed up and had enough. Uprisings sprung up all over the country, resulting in an all-out civil war between Gaddafi loyalists and anti-government rebels trying to suppress Gaddafi's power.

Months into heated gun battles, Gaddafi and his close family members fled to the country's western part. NATO began to support the rebel forces by bombing cities that supported Gaddafi loyalists' strongholds. A no-fly zone crushed any air support Gaddafi would need and also prevented him from fleeing the country. More and more countries began recognizing the rebel-backed governing body. Gaddafi, now a wanted man, went into hiding carrying his most prized weapon, a 9mm Browning plated in solid gold and decorated with an elaborate floral pattern.

Several months passed with no sign of Gaddafi's whereabouts until multiple rumors broke in the summer of 2011 he had been killed. By this point, most of Libya was burning and war-torn due to oil fields set ablaze in Gaddafi's defiance. Libya held an average of 133 tons of gold bars in its reserves before chaos ensued in the country, but that gold could do nothing to stop Gaddafi's demise.

Grainy video footage allowed the world to witness a bloodied pleading Gaddafi in his final moments, although the footage did not show how he died. A dictator who ruled for forty-two years and survived several assassination attempts was finally worn down to a nub by war with his people. What he was clutching after being found hiding in a drainage pipe took on its own story. Gaddafi's gun, the gold 9mm Browning, was being passed around by the rebels that captured him before one rebel was hoisted on the shoulders of several men and held high as a symbol of victory for a new Libya.

The infamous pistol disappeared after the war was over, and took *BBC* foreign correspondent Gabriel Gatehouse five years to rediscover its whereabouts again. A man named Mohammed Elbibi found the gun after Gaddafi's surrender and became an accidental hero of the revolution. He even remembered Gabriel taking his picture with the famed pistol in 2011 when he was seventeen years old. Gaddafi's gold gun was finally proven to still exist and remains in safekeeping but at a deadly cost.

It turns out on the 32nd anniversary of Gaddafi's rule, the gold pistol was given to him as a gift from one of his sons, so it holds great significance and symbolism to Gaddafi loyalists. Libya's power vacuum after Gaddafi's removal has made it an even more dangerous place with terror groups like ISIS and rivals taking hold, still grappling for the right to be the sole ruler of Libya. Another rebel by Omran Shabaan was photographed holding the pistol and later was captured, beaten, and tortured by Gaddafi loyalists in 2012. Omran was rescued but died from his injuries at a hospital days later.

This gives the gun's current owner Mohammed Elbibi good reason to be cautious about having such a controversial item in his possession. He has received numerous death threats and tries to keep a low profile in Libya out of fear. In an interview with *BBC* journalist Gabriel Gatehouse, he demands to have his name cleared of how he came upon owning Gaddafi's infamous gold gun" Please tell the world it was not me who killed Gaddafi," he says. Did he imagine that, nearly five years later, Libya would still be at war with itself? "I did not," he says. "I am really sad about that. When I see Libyans killing Libyans, it's too bad. Everybody wants to be like Gaddafi."

The process of gold-plating guns isn't difficult and could be done by anyone with easily purchased tools. There are even YouTube videos that describe the process. The gun is first broken down and thoroughly cleaned. Second, a coat of copper is applied by a special brush to the parts as a base. Finally, the gold plate is brushed on, and the part is dipped in water. Now, put the gun back together, and that's it, you're done. -War is Boring

When the dust clears, it's evident that gold and dictatorship have some weird connection to guns, and Gaddafi is a perfect example. It looks like the world will see many more items plated in gold thanks to the internet but affording the gold to even plate something as obnoxious as a gun is usually accompanied by large sums of cash that most times only a drug lord or dictator would have. More interesting stories like Muammar al-Gaddafi's gold gun will continue to amaze readers in the future as long as dictators and criminals build their foundations on war, power, and money. Gold guns and the violent men that wield them won't be far behind.

CORRUPTION IN VENEZUELA BLOOD & GOLD

Venezuela during the early years of president Hugo Chavez reign economically looked much better than it does today. The South American country saw limited prosperity, the largest oil reserves in the world and tons of gold bullion in its banks. Fast forward to 2019 and Venezuela bears the scars of years of mismanagement, crime, corruption, and unemployment that has spiraled the country into chaos. An excerpt from *The Guardian* explains Venezuela oil-rich grand opening and grand closing "Chávez had the good fortune to preside over the biggest oil boom in the country's history. He is still revered by half the population, who recalls his social programs and popular touch. But by the time he died of cancer in 2013 he had bankrupted his country, running up debt and strangling the private sector."

In the wake of Chávez death political tension between current President Nicolas Maduro and opposition leader Juan Guaido has caused growing unrest and a possible humanitarian crisis as millions flee the country. During the descent of government gold has become the single most important thing to own and very well could save people's lives trying to avoid the political tug of war between Maduro and Guaido. Investor *Frank Holmes* explains the importance of having gold ownership in moments of absolute fear and unrest. "My point in bringing this up is to reinforce the importance of gold's Fear Trade, which says that demand for the yellow metal rises when inflation threatens to destroy a nation's currency—as it's doing right now in Venezuela. A Venezuelan family that had the prudence to store some of its wealth in gold would be in a much better position today to survive or escape President Maduro's corrupt, far-left regime."

Due to sanctions from the United States, the Venezuelan government is also strapped for cash. The Bolivar which is Venezuela's premier banknote has essentially become worthless in a matter of few weeks forcing Maduro to act drastically. "Venezuela's socialist president Nicolas Maduro—who only this past weekend survived an assassination attempt involving several explosive-laden drones—announced recently that the country plans to rein in hyperinflation by lopping off five zeroes from its currency." Dropping value of your currency is a disastrous sign and things appear to only be getting worse for those clinging to power in Venezuela.

Venezuela, home to the world's largest oil reserves, is a case study in the perils of petrol statehood. Since its discovery in the 1920s, oil has taken Venezuela on an exhilarating but dangerous boom-and-bust ride that offers lessons for other resource-rich states. Decades of poor governance have driven what was once one of Latin America's most prosperous countries to economic and political ruin. - Rocio Cara Labrador

Maduro has already tapped into the central bank selling off tons of the precious gold to countries like China, Turkey and Russian against the agreement of countries like France, Spain, and The United States after Maduro declined to hold new elections and receive much-needed aid from outside sources. The future of the petrol state of South America will be based on its people ability to stabilize and remove the corrupt politicians. Making a game plan to revive the economy past its boom and bust cycles will be its citizens best bet of revival. As it currently stands Maduro is in charge of those decisions and selling up to 40% of Venezuela's gold reserves in a year to support his destructive regime is Juan Guaido's evidence of his outrageous spending and incompetence as a leader. This type of slander against Maduro is common in the political climate and clearly isn't affecting Maduro or his control over the country.

In the early spring of 2019, President Donald Trump has stepped up his effort to slow down Maduro's corrupt gold consumption by freezing any assets of Venezuelan state-run mining company Minerven. The United States has prohibited any dealings with the South American mining giant and halted any business transactions the company may have with U.S controlled territories abroad. A spokesperson from the U.S. Treasury told the *Wall Street Journal* why such heavy sanctions have been placed on Venezuelan gold. "The U.S. said the gold operations have been another way the Maduro government has tapped the state's resources for personal gain and to launder proceeds from corruption, drug trafficking, and other illicit operations."

Heavier sanctions may arise in the future if a resolution isn't quickly sought but gold seems to be the focal point for Maduro by any means. The country is in disarray as it continues to default on bonds and break promises with creditors. "A Venezuela bondholder pulled the country into a U.S. court over its massive bond default, signaling that creditors are tiring of waiting for a political change that could allow for restructuring negotiations. London-based Pharo Management LLC sued in New York state Supreme Court on Friday for $26 million in overdue payments, marking down the first known lawsuit surrounding Venezuela's sovereign debt default from a well-known asset manager in the U.S."

Corruption has always been rampant in Venezuelan politics but the country is torn between democracy and dictatorship. Elections were held and after Nicolas Maduro claimed the presidency for another six years angered citizens pursued a failed coup led by Juan Guaido a bitter rival to Maduro. Many other dark events involving gold and corruption such as police brutality at anti-government rallies, women being forced to sell their bodies to eat and Venezuelan citizens fleeing the country to places like Trinidad and Tobago adds to the list of the country's internal breakdown. It is too early to tell whether the country will fall into all-out civil war, a socialist dictatorship or go broke once it runs out of gold but what it does show is years of greed, fast profits in oil and gold don't mix without a backup plan.

APPENDIX

Cover Me In Gold required extensive research which relied on the work of many authors, periodicals and informational sources from the internet, texts, and economic professionals. The various chapters and footnotes reference the information I found to have a particular interest in gold, silver, socioeconomic history or assisted in bringing valuable research to create the completion of this book. The biggest error a thinking person can make is to believe that one particular version of history is absolute fact. History is made up by multiple observers and this book is no different. A more complete list of my citations can be found in the Bibliography.

The End

BIBLIOGRAPHY

THE STATE OF THE GOLD INDUSTRY. (2018). Retrieved from thisisgold.co.za: http://www.thisisgold.co.za/component/jdownloads/send/2-fact-sheets/19-the-state-of-the-gold-industry

Academy, S. (2012). *Overview of the Federal Reserve* . Retrieved from Saylor.org: http://www.saylor.org/site/wp-content/uploads/2012/09/SAYLOR.ORG-ECON302-Chapter-1.pdf

Academy, S. (2012). *Principals of Economics* . Retrieved from Saylor.org:
http://www.saylor.org/site/textbooks/Principles%20of%20Economics.pdf

Academy, W. R. (2013). *Most expensive shirt: Datta Phuge breaks Guinness world record*. Retrieved from https://www.worldrecordacademy.com/business/most_expensive_shirt_Datta_Phuge_breaks_Guinness_world_record_213462.html

Ahamed, L. (2009). *Lords of Finance: The Bankers who Broke the World.* Penguin Books.

Alexandra Irving, J. A. (n.d.). Hidden Treasure from the Royal Cemetery at Ur: Technology Sheds New Light on the Ancient Near East.

Alexandra Wexler, T. N. (2018). *South Africa Gold-Mining Compa-*

nies Pay High Price to Keep Digging. Retrieved from wsj.com: https://www.wsj.com/articles/south-africa-gold-mining-companies-pay-high-price-to-keep-digging-1538920800?ns=prod/accounts-wsj

AMADEO, K. (2019). *History of the Gold Standard*. Retrieved from thebalance.com: https://www.thebalance.com/what-is-the-history-of-the-gold-standard-3306136

Anderson, C. (1994). *Black Labor, White Wealth.* Duncan & Duncan Inc.

Anderson, C. (1997). *Dirty Little Secrets About Black History : Its Heroes & Other Troublemakers.* Powernomics Corp of Amer.

Anderson, C. (2017). *Colloidal Silver: The Poor Man's Antibiotic.* Retrieved from DiscoveryWorld: https://www.discoveryworld.us/science/colloidal-silver-the-poor-mans-antibiotic/

Anderson, L. ((Online)). *Conspicuous Consumption*. Retrieved from Slate.com: http://www.slate.com/articles/health_and_science/explainer/2012/07/the_666_gold_wrapped_douche_burger_is_it_safe_to_eat_gold_.html

Anglogoldashanti. (2017). *MEET OUR METAL: GOLD*. Retrieved from Anglogoldashanti.com: https://www.anglogoldashanti.-com/meet-our-metal-gold/

Anne Marie Helmenstine, P. (n.d.). *ThoughtCo*. Retrieved from 10 Interesting Gold Facts (Online): https://www.thoughtco.com/interesting-gold-facts-607641

Arielle P. Kozloff, B. M. (1992). *Egypt's Dazzling Sun: Amenhotep III and His World.* Cleveland Museum of Art Bookstore; 1st Edition.

Aristotle. (340 BC). *Teachings.* Stagira: Self Published.

Ash, A. (2018). *China's 2018 Gold Buying: Half-Empty, Half-Full.* Retrieved from Bullionvault.com: https://www.bullionvault.-com/gold-news/china-gold-030820184

ASSOCIATION, T. A. (n.d.). *ARCHIVES OF THE AMERICAN DENTAL ASSOCIATION FAQS ON THE HISTORY OF DENTISTRY.* Retrieved from ada.org: https://www.ada.org/~/media/ADA/Education%20and%20Careers/Files/faq_dentistry.pdf?la=en

Ayensu, E. S. (1998). *Ashanti Gold: The African Legacy of the World's Most Precious Metal.* Marshall Editions; First Edition edition.

BARTOK, M. (2009). *Striking it rich on the Izu Peninsula*. Retrieved from Japantimes.co.jp: https://www.japantimes.co.jp/life/2009/08/16/travel/striking-it-rich-on-the-izu-peninsula/#.XFxJBy-ZPVo

BEATTIE, A. (2009). *Silver Thursday: How Two Wealthy Traders Cornered The Market*. Retrieved from Investopedia.com: https://www.investopedia.com/articles/optioninvestor/09/silver-thursday-hunt-brothers.asp

Bernstein, P. L. (2000). The Power of Gold: The History of An Obsession. In P. L. Bernstein, *The Power of Gold: The History of An Obsession.* John Wiley and Sons, inc.

Blakemore, E. (2018). *The Enslaved Native Americans Who Made The Gold Rush Possible*. Retrieved from History.com: https://www.history.com/news/the-enslaved-native-americans-who-made-the-gold-rush-possible

Boeckmann, C. (2017). *BIRTHSTONES BY MONTH: MEANINGS AND COLORS*. Retrieved from Almanac.com: https://www.almanac.com/content/birthstones-and-their-meanings

Boekeloo, L. (n.d.). *Jewelry and the Astrological Signs*. Retrieved from Streetdirectory.com: https://www.streetdirectory.com/travel_guide/61973/jewelry/jewelry_and_the_astrological_signs.html

Boots, T. (2005). *Get Rich or Die Trying Meet the original 50 Cent-the gangster who inspired the biggest name in rap.* Retrieved from web.archive.org: https://web.archive.org/web/20070929131729/http://www.stuffmagazine.com/articles/index.aspx?id=1112

Boring, W. i. (2019). *What Do Hitler, Saddam Hussein and Gaddafi Have In Common? They Loved Golden Guns.* Retrieved from Nationalinterest.org: https://nationalinterest.org/blog/buzz/what-do-hitler-saddam-hussein-and-gaddafi-have-common-they-loved-golden-guns-48792

Bortolot, A. (2000). *Gold in Asante Courtly Arts.* Retrieved from https://www.metmuseum.org/toah/hd/asan_2/hd_asan_2.htm

Bovill, E. (1969). *Caravans of the old sahara and the gold trade of the Moors.* Oxford University Press.

Bowdich, T. E. (2014). *Mission from Cape Coast Castle to Ashantee With a Statistical Account of that Kingdom, and Geographical Notices of Other Parts of the Interior of Afric.* Cambridge University Press.

Brands, H. (2003). *The Age of Gold: The California Gold Rush and the New American Dream.* Anchor Publishing .

BRIGHT, D. R. (1986). *Language of the Cells.* Dr. Robert C. Bright D.C. Retrieved from goldgold.com: http://www.goldgold.com/gold-and-how-it-affects-the-body.html

Britannica, T. E. (2019). *Midas GREEK MYTHOLOGY.* Retrieved from britannica.com: https://www.britannica.com/topic/Midas-Greek-mythology

Britannica, T. E. (2019). *Pedro de Alvarado.* Retrieved from Britannica.com: https://www.britannica.com/biography/Pedro-de-Alvarado#ref898514

Bureau of Labor Statistics, U. D. (2013). *Gold prices rise more than 100 percent since 2008* . Retrieved from bls.gov: https://www.bls.-gov/opub/ted/2013/ted_20130305.htm

Bureau, U. S. (2019). *Government Confiscation of Gold: Understanding the Facts.* Retrieved from invest.usgoldbureau.com: https://invest.us-goldbureau.com/gold-confiscation

Bureau, U. S. (n.d.). *Government Confiscation of Gold: Understanding the Facts.* Retrieved from https://invest.usgoldbureau.com/gold-confiscation

Burns, C. (2017). *Montezuma's Golden Treasure.* Retrieved from life-ofadventure.com: https://www.lifeofadventure.com/montezumas-gold/

Cahalan, S. (2018). *Mining for asteroids will be the next gold rush.* Retrieved from Nypost.com: https://nypost.com/2018/02/24/min-ing-for-asteroids-will-be-the-next-gold-rush/

Carlton, G. (n.d.). *The Roman Emperor Who Might Have Died By Having Molten Gold Poured Down His Throat.* Retrieved from Ranker.-com: https://www.ranker.com/list/life-of-emperor-valerian-after-being-conquered/genevieve-carlton

Carmichael, J. (1993). *African Eldorado - Gold Coast to Ghana.* Gerald Duckworth & Co. Ltd.

Cartwright, M. (2013). *Marcus Licinius Crassus*. Retrieved from Ancient.eu: https://www.ancient.eu/Marcus_Licinius_Crassus/

Chambers, M. (1985, February 28). *GOETZ SPOKE TO ONE YOUTH, THEN SHOT AGAIN, POLICE SAY*. Retrieved from New York Times : https://www.nytimes.com/1985/02/28/nyregion/goetz-spoke-to-one-youth-then-shot-again-police-say.html

Che, X. (2013). *Death Mask of Agamemnon*. Retrieved from Ancient.eu: https://www.ancient.eu/image/1235/death-mask-of-agamemnon/

Chen, A. (2018). *Why failing to recycle electronics leaves gold mines untapped*. Retrieved from Theverge.com: https://www.theverge.com/2018/4/23/17270960/electronic-waste-urban-mining-materials-recycling

Christopher, G. (2014). *Warning: 3 Billion People Covet Your Gold... Is China Buying Up All the Gold?* Retrieved from Moneymetals.com: https://www.moneymetals.com/news/2014/09/24/warning-3-billion-people-covet-your-gold-000607

Clark, J. (2017). *Risks of Investing in Numismatic Coins – GoldSilver*. Retrieved from Goldsilver.com: https://goldsilver.com/blog/investor-beware-numismatic-collector-coins/

Clark, J. (2019). *The 3 Flaws: Why the Hunt Bros Were Not the Primary Reason for Silver's 1970s Spike*. Retrieved from Goldsilver.com: https://goldsilver.com/blog/the-3-flaws-why-the-hunt-bros-were-not-the-primary-reason-for-silvers-1970s-spike/

Company, I. M. (2019). *What connects gold and baby hair?* Retrieved from sciencefocus.com: https://www.sciencefocus.com/the-human-body/what-connects-gold-and-baby-hair/

Complex. (2011). *The 50 greatest chains in hip-hop*. Retrieved from Complex.com: https://www.complex.com/style/2011/12/the-50-greatest-chains-in-hip-hop/52

Cookson, C. (2018). *Scientists discover the origins of gold in space*. Retrieved from Financial Times: https://www.ft.com/content/15d33cc8-c3c4-11e7-b30e-a7c1c7c13aab

Copping, J. (n.d.). *Explorers hot on the trail of Atahualpa and the Treasure of the Llanganates*. Retrieved from telegraph.co.uk:

https://www.telegraph.co.uk/news/worldnews/southamerica/ecuador/10517904/Explorers-hot-on-the-trail-of-Atahualpa-and-the-Treasure-of-the-Llanganates.html

Council, W. G. (2019). *Buying physical gold (bars and coins).* Retrieved from Gold.org: https://www.gold.org/what-we-do/investing-gold/how-buy-gold/bars-and-coins

Council, W. G. (2019). *Gold-backed ETFs and similar.* Retrieved from Gold.org: https://www.gold.org/what-we-do/investing-gold/how-buy-gold/gold-backed-etfs-and-similar

Crystal vaults. (n.d.). *Your On-Line Guide to The Healing Energies, Metaphysical Properties, Legendary Uses and Meaning of Diamond.* Retrieved from Crystalvaults.com: https://www.crystalvaults.com/crystal-encyclopedia/diamond

Dass, R. R. (n.d.). *The Spanish Unraveling Of the Incan Empire: The Importance of Fibers and Textiles of the Past.* Retrieved from Wisconsin.edu: https://minds.wisconsin.edu/bitstream/handle/1793/75764/

Dean, S. (2018). *These Bacteria Digest Toxic Metals And Poop Out Tiny Gold Nuggets.* Retrieved from Science Alert : https://www.sciencealert.com/bacteria-produce-gold-nuggets-cupriavidus-metallidurans

Demarco, A. (2011). *Harry Winston Sales Up 44%, Profits Fall 23%.* Retrieved from Forbes.com: https://www.forbes.com/sites/anthonydemarco/2011/09/07/harry-winston-sales-up-44-profits-fall-23/#67cc428326ae

Department of the Arts of Africa, O. a. (2000, October). *The Trans-Saharan Gold Trade (7th–14th Century Century.* Retrieved from https://www.metmuseum.org/toah/hd/gold/hd_gold.htm

Dhwty. (2015). *This Day in History: Pizarro traps Inca emperor Atahualpa.* Retrieved from http://www.history.com/this-day-in-history/pizarro-traps-Inca-emperor-atahualpa

Diehl, P. N. (2016, February 26). *The Real Diehl – An Unclassified Peek Inside the Fort Knox Gold Depository.* Retrieved from CoinWeek: https://coinweek.com/bullion-report/the-real-diehl-an-unclassified-peek-inside-fort-knox-gold-depository/

Dirkmaat, O. (2018). *Why Gold Prices Fell In 2008.* Retrieved from

Goldrepublic.com: https://www.goldrepublic.com/news/why-gold-prices-fell-in-2008

Documents of Freedom:History, G. &. (n.d.). *Popular Sovereignty and the Consent of the Governed.* Retrieved from docsoffreedom.org: https://www.docsoffreedom.org/student/readings/popular-sovereignty-and-the-consent-of-the-governed

Editors, B. (2014). *Muammar al-Qaddafi Biography.* Retrieved from The Biography.com: https://www.biography.com/people/muammar-al-qaddafi-39014

Els, F. (2017). *World's deepest mine gets $1 billion injection.* Retrieved from Mining.com: http://www.mining.com/worlds-deepest-mine-gets-1-billion-injection/

Everythingchopsticks. (2013). *All About Silver Chopsticks.* Retrieved from Everythingchopsticks.com: https://everythingchopsticks.-com/All-About-Silver-Chopsticks

Fandom. (2019). *Leprechaun.* Retrieved from Fandom.com: https://characters.fandom.com/wiki/Leprechaun

Fernie, W. T. (1973). *The Occult and Curative Powers of Precious Stones.* Blauvelt, NY: Rudolph Steiner Publications.

Fessenden, M. (Online). *How doctors are harnessing the power of gold to fight cancer.* Retrieved from SmithsonianMag.com: https://www.-smithsonianmag.com/innovation/how-doctors-harnessing-power-gold-fight-cancer-180949436/?no-ist

Foundation, T. S. (2014). *Esoteric Truth about Gold.* Retrieved from Youtube.com: https://www.youtube.com/watch?v=SQtJUzpVcIM

France-Presse, A. (2016). *Indian businessman famed for $240,000 gold shirt 'beaten to death'.* Retrieved from theguardian.com: https://www.theguardian.com/world/2016/jul/16/indian-businessman-famed-for-240000-gold-shirt-beaten-to-death

Franco, V. (n.d.). *What is the Meaning of Jewelry for the Inca Culture in Peru?* Retrieved from USAToday.com: https://traveltips.usatoday.-com/meaning-jewelry-inca-culture-peru-30252.html

Gabriel Tolliver, R. O. (n.d.). *Bling: The Hip-hop Jewellery Book* (Vol. 2006). Bloomsbury Publishing PLC.

Gale, T. (2008). *Gold, God, And Glory.* Retrieved from Encyclopedia.com: https://www.encyclopedia.com/social-sciences/applied-and-social-sciences-magazines/gold-god-and-glory

Ganz, D. (2009). *Gold all there when Ft. Knox opened doors*. Retrieved from https://www.numismaticnews.net/article/Gold_al-l_there_when_Ft_Knox_opened_doors

Gatehouse, G. (2016). *My search for Gaddafi's golden gun*. Retrieved from bbc.com: https://www.bbc.com/news/magazine-35466077

Gateway, B. (Online). *Bible Gateway*. Retrieved from Biblica. Exodus 25 (Online): https://www.biblegateway.com/passage/?search=Exodus+25&version=NIV

Gateway., B. (n.d.). *Exodus 25:1-7 NIV*. Retrieved from Bible Gateway.: https://www.biblegateway.com/passage/?search=Exodus+25%3A1-7&version=NIV

Genius. (n.d.). *Jay-z Politics as usual Lyrics*. Retrieved from Genius.-com: https://genius.com/Jay-z-politics-as-usual-lyrics

Gold Facts. (2018). Retrieved from sciencekids.co.nz: http://www.-sciencekids.co.nz/sciencefacts/metals/gold.html

GoldApple, L. (2017). *Destroy your phone Closing the Loop*. Retrieved from Atlasofthefuture.org: https://atlasofthefuture.org/project/closing-the-loop/

Goldman, D. (2016). *Apple Recovered 2,204 pounds of gold from broken iphones last year*. Retrieved from CNN.com: https://money.cnn.-com/2016/04/15/technology/apple-gold-recycling/

Golubova, A. (2018). *The Next Gold Rush Is Not Cryptos, But 'Outer Space Gold Mines'*. Retrieved from Kitco.com: https://www.kitco.-com/news/2018-02-27/The-Next-Gold-Rush-Is-Not-Cryptos-But-Outer-Space-Gold-Mines-Famed-Physicist.html

Graber, C. (2011). *Farming Like the Incas*. Retrieved from Smithsonianmag.com: https://www.smithsonianmag.com/history/farming-like-the-incas-70263217/

Greekmythology.com. (2019). *King Midas* . Retrieved from Greekmythology.com: https://www.greekmythology.com/Myths/Mortals/King_Midas/king_midas.html

Green, T. (n.d.). *Ages of Gold* (Vol. 2007). GFMS Limited .

Greenburg, Z. O. (2019). *Inside Nipsey Hussle's Blueprint To*

Become A Real Estate Mogul. Retrieved from forbes.com: https://www.forbes.com/sites/zackomalleygreenburg/2019/02/20/nipsey-hussle-opportunity-zone-real-estate-mogul-blueprint/#70eaaf696364

Greever, W. S. (1963). *The Bonanza West: The Story of the Western Mining Rushes.* Norman: University of Oklahoma Press.

Griggs, M. B. (2017). *ACE Neutron star collisions may have created most of the gold in the universe.* Retrieved from Popsci.com: https://www.popsci.com/neutron-star-gold

HANDWERK, B. (2005). *Egypt's 'King Tut Curse' Caused by Tomb Toxins?* Retrieved from Nationalgeographic.com: https://www.nationalgeographic.com/science/2005/05/news-tutankhamun-carnarvon-mold-bacteria-toxins/

Harris, J. (2013). *The 10 Most Stylish Drug Kingpins of All Time.* Retrieved from Complex.com: https://www.complex.com/style/2013/01/the-10-most-stylish-drug-kingpins-of-all-time/pablo-escobar

Hart, M. (2014). *Gold: The Race for the World's Most Seductive Metal.* Simon & Schuster.

Hernandez, D. (2019). *The Hunt for Alien Life Starts in Earth's Most Extreme Places.* Retrieved from wsj.com: https://www.wsj.com/articles/the-hunt-for-alien-life-starts-in-earths-most-extreme-places-11554810637?mod=searchresults&page=1&pos=1

Hill, J. (2014). Retrieved from Ancient Egypt Online: https://ancientegyptonline.co.uk/jewellerycollar/

Hill, M. (2009). *The Spread of Islam in West Africa: Containment, Mixing, and Reform from the Eighth to the Twentieth Century.* Retrieved from https://spice.fsi.stanford.edu/docs/the_spread_of_islam_in_west_africa_containment_mixing_and_reform_from_the_eighth_to_the_twentieth_century/

History.com. (n.d.). *Pizarro Executes Last Inca Emperor.* Retrieved from history.com: https://www.history.com/this-day-in-history/pizarro-executes-last-inca-emperor

Holmes, F. (2011). *From Spacecrafts To Temples: The Amazing Uses Of Gold.* Retrieved from businessinsider.com: https://www.businessinsider.com/from-spacecrafts-to-temples-the-amazing-uses-of-gold-2011-8

Holmes, F. (2017). *Germans Have Quietly Become the World's Biggest Buyers of Gold*. Retrieved from Usfunds.com: http://www.usfunds.-com/investor-library/frank-talk/germans-have-quietly-become-the-worlds-biggest-buyers-of-gold/#.XHRCwy-ZPR0

Holmes, F. (2018). *Gold, World War II and Operation Fish*. Retrieved from Usfunds.com: http://www.usfunds.com/investor-library/frank-talk/gold-world-war-ii-and-operation-fish/#.XGjrNy-ZPVo

Holmes, F. (2018). *Wait Until You See the Price of Gold in Venezuela Right Now*. Retrieved from Usfunds.com: http://www.usfunds.-com/investor-library/frank-talk/wait-until-you-see-the-price-of-gold-in-venezuela-right-now/#.XIVfRS-ZPR1

Horne, L. (1998). *Ur and Its Treasures The Royal Tombs*. Retrieved from Penn museum: https://www.penn.museum/sites/expedition/ur-and-its-treasures/

Houston, D. (2018). *Gold: Meanings, Properties and Powers*. Retrieved from https://meanings.crystalsandjewelry.com/gold/

Houston, D. (2018). *Silver: Meanings, Properties, and Powers.* Retrieved from Crystalsandjewelry.com: https://meanings.crystal-sandjewelry.com/silver/

Hulick, K. (2017). The Chemistry of Everyday Elements: Gold . In K. Hulick, *The Chemistry of Everyday Elements: Gold* (p. 13). Mason Crest.

Hussle, N. (2018). *Victory Lap*. Retrieved from genius.com: https://genius.com/Nipsey-hussle-victory-lap-lyrics

Ian Talley, L. R. (2019). *As Treasury Sanctions Venezuela Gold Miner, Trump Says U.S. Can Do More*. Retrieved from wsj.com: https://www.wsj.com/articles/u-s-sanctions-venezuelas-state-gold-mining-company-11553009666

Ibis Communication. (2019). *Dining With Attila the Hun, 448 AD* . Retrieved from eyewitnesstohistory.com: http://www.eyewitnessto-history.com/attila.htm

Innes, E. (2013). *Nose drops made my skin to turn SILVER': Woman suffers with condition for 60 years after the metal built up in her body.*

Retrieved from Dailymail.co.uk: https://www.dailymail.co.uk/health/article-2522463/Woman-suffers-argyria-60-years-silver-built-body.html

Innes, R. H. (2019). *Hernan Cortes*. Retrieved from Britannica: https://www.britannica.com/biography/Hernan-Cortes

Investers, U. G. (2019). *The Many Uses of Gold Dentistry:*. Retrieved from usfunds.com: http://www.usfunds.com/slideshows/the-many-uses-of-gold/#.XJD15C-ZNsM

Ivan. (2019). *Why Was Gold So Important To The Ancient Anunnaki?* Retrieved from ancient-code.com: https://www.ancient-code.com/gold-and-the-importance-to-the-anunnaki/

Jeff Clark, S. M. (2015). *Gold & Silver Confiscation: Can the Government Seize Assets?* Retrieved from Goldsilver.com: https://goldsilver.com/blog/gold-confiscation-history-myths-and-real-solutions/

John, T. (2017). *The New Gold Rush for Our e-Waste*. Retrieved from Time.com: http://time.com/4970288/mitsubishi-gold-rush-for-ewaste/

Jones, R. S. (1973). *Gold Content of Water, Plants, and Animals.* GE0L0GICAL SURVEY CIRCULAR. GE0L0GICAL SURVEY CIRCULAR.

Jones, S. (2005). *Stan Jones*. Retrieved from ontheissues.org: http://ontheissues.org/Senate/Stan_Jones.htm

KENTON, W. (2018). *Irrational Exuberance*. Retrieved from Investopedia.com: https://www.investopedia.com/terms/i/irrationalexuberance.asp

Khandelwal, P. (2018). *20kg gold, 21 luxury cars, team of bouncers: Golden Baba in Ghaziabad on last leg of Kanwar yatra*. Retrieved from Hindustantimes.com: https://www.hindustantimes.com/cities/20kg-gold-21-luxury-cars-team-of-bouncers-golden-baba-in-ghaziabad-on-last-leg-of-kanwar-yatra/story-jPr4g0eJkOyHWy-KYAARylK.html

kidsplayandcreate. (2019). *leprechaun facts for kids*. Retrieved from kidsplayandcreate.com: https://www.kidsplayandcreate.com/leprechaun-facts-for-kids/

King, H. M. (2019). *Uses of Gold in Electronics*. Retrieved from Geology.com: https://geology.com/minerals/gold/uses-of-gold.shtml#electronics

Klepper, M., & Gunther, M. (1996). *The Wealthy 100: From Benjamin Franklin to Bill Gates—A Ranking of the Richest Americans, Past and Present,*. Carol Publishing Group,.

Knapp, B. (1996). *Copper, Silver and Gold* . Atlantic Europe Publishing .

KOREN, M. (2017). *The Plume of Gold Ejected by a Cosmic Collision.* Retrieved from Theatlantic.com: https://www.theatlantic.com/science/archive/2017/10/the-making-of-cosmic-bling/543030/

Labrador, R. C. (2019). *Venezuela: The Rise and Fall of a Petrostate.* Retrieved from cfr.org: https://www.cfr.org/backgrounder/venezuela-crisis

Labs, E. (2004). *The Return of Silver in Medicine: Colloidal Silver - Nature's Alternative to Antibiotics".* Retrieved from EMR Labs: https://www.quantumbalancing.com/news/cs_return.htm

LAL, P. (n.d.). *Follow these rules while wearing gold to attract wealth.* Retrieved from Speakingtree: https://www.speakingtree.in/allslides/follow-these-rules-while-wearing-gold-to-attract-wealth

Lassiter, M. D. (2015). Impossible Criminals: The Suburban Imperatives of America's War on Drugs. *Journal of American History,* , 126–140. Retrieved from academic.oup.com: https://academic.oup.com/jah/article/102/1/126/686691

Layden, L. (2018). *Banks fell in the Great Recession, but they're stronger now.* Retrieved from usatoday.com: https://www.usatoday.com/story/money/2018/03/14/banks-fell-great-recession-but-theyre-stronger-now/394354002/

Levy, B. (2009). *Conquistador: Hernan Cortes, King Montezuma, and the Last Stand of the Aztecs.* Bantam.

LIOUDIS, N. K. (2019). *What is the Gold Standard?* Retrieved from Investopedia.com: https://www.investopedia.com/ask/answers/09/gold-standard.asp

Lloyd, A. (1965). *The drums of Kumasi: the story of the Ashanti wars.* London, UK: Longmans.

Lloyd, E. (2016). *How The Hyksos Invasion Of Ancient Egypt Changed*

History. Retrieved from Ancientpages.com: http://www.ancient-pages.com/2016/10/26/hyksos-invasion-ancient-egypt-changed-history/

Lunney, D. (Online). *Where does gold come from?* Retrieved from ed.ted.com: https://ed.ted.com/lessons/where-does-gold-come-from-david-lunney

MacQuarrie, K. (2008). *The Last Days of the Incas.* Simon & Schuster.

Maloney, M. (2015). *Guide To Investing in Gold & Silver: Protect Your Financial Future.* WealthCycle Press.

Marinersmuseum. (n.d.). *Francisco Pizarro*. Retrieved from Exploration.marinersmuseum.org: https://exploration.marinersmuseum.org/subject/francisco-pizarro/

Matonis, J. (2009). *Hunt Brothers Demanded Physical Delivery Too.* Retrieved from themonetaryfuture.blogspot.com: http://themonetaryfuture.blogspot.com/2009/01/hunt-brothers-demanded-physical.html

Mayerowitz, S. (2008). *Welcome to the World's Largest Gold Vault* . Retrieved from ABCNews.com: https://abcnews.go.com/Business/story?id=5835433&page=1

McCarthy, J. (2014). *A gold obsession pays dividends for Indian women.* Retrieved from NPR.com: https://www.npr.org/sections/parallels/2014/04/14/301412384/a-gold-obsession-pays-dividends-for-indian-women

McGrath, D. R. (2012). *The Silver Kings*. Retrieved from Irishamerica.com: https://irishamerica.com/2012/09/the-silver-kings/

McLAUGHLIN, P. H. (2013). *The Origin of Gold.* Retrieved from Goldgold.com: http://www.goldgold.com/the-origin-of-gold.html

Melody, J. G. (1995). *Love Is in the Earth: A Kaleidoscope of Crystals: The Reference Book Describing the Metaphysical Properties of the Mineral Kingdom.* Earth Love Pub House; Updated, 3rd edition .

Meredith, M. (2015). *The Fortunes of Africa.* New York; Public Affairs.

Meredith, S. (2019). *Forget oil: Here's why gold is key to Venezuela's crisis-stricken government*. Retrieved from MSN.com: https://www.msn.com/en-us/money/markets/forget-oil-heres-why-gold-is-key-to-venezuelas-crisis-stricken-government/ar-BBTa7FL

Metmuseum. (2000). *The Trans-Saharan Gold Trade (7th–14th Century).* (D. o. Africa, Producer) Retrieved from Metmuseum.org: https://www.metmuseum.org/toah/hd/gold/hd_gold.htm

Minster, C. (2017). *Biography of Atahualpa, Last King of the Inca.* Retrieved from Thoughtco.com: https://www.thoughtco.com/biography-of-atahualpa-king-of-inca-2136541

Minster, C. (2017). *The Capture of Inca Atahualpa.* Retrieved from https://www.thoughtco.com/capture-of-inca-atahualpa-2136546

Minster, C. (2018). *10 Facts About Dona 'La Malinche' Marina The Woman Who Betrayed the Aztecs.* Retrieved from Thoughtco.com: https://www.thoughtco.com/facts-about-dona-marina-malinche-2136536

Minster, C. (2018). *Ten Facts About Montezuma.* Retrieved from thoughtco.com: https://www.thoughtco.com/ten-facts-about-montezuma-2136263

Mint, R. (2019). *Isaac Newton.* Retrieved from royalmintmuseum.org.uk: http://www.royalmintmuseum.org.uk/history/people/mint-officials/isaac-newton/index.html

Mirror, M. (2016). Retrieved from mumbaimirror.indiatimes.com: https://mumbaimirror.indiatimes.com/mumbai/crime/I-saw-them-attack-dad-and-smash-his-head-with-a-stone/articleshow/53234971.cms

MIZOKAMI, K. (2013). *The Men With the Golden Guns.* Retrieved from warisboring.com: https://warisboring.com/the-men-with-the-golden-guns/

Molly Oldfield, J. M. (Online). *Quite interesting facts about gold.* Retrieved from Telegraph.Co.Uk: https://www.telegraph.co.uk/men/the-filter/qi/8667421/QI-Quite-interesting-facts-about-gold.html

Montet, P. (1951). *La necropole royale de Tanis I: Les constructions et le tombeau de Psoussennes a Tanis.*

Morgan. (n.d.). *Lost History* (Vol. 2007). Washington D.C.: National Geographic Society.

Moy, E. (2014). *Is There Gold in Fort Knox?* Retrieved from https://www.newsmax.com/t/finance/article/575519/221

Museum, P. (2018). *QUEEN PUABI'S HEADDRESS.* Retrieved from Penn.museum: https://www.penn.museum/collections/highlights/neareast/puabi.php

Nationalww2museum. (2019). *Research Starters: Worldwide Deaths in World War II.* Retrieved from Nationalww2museum.org: https://www.nationalww2museum.org/students-teachers/student-resources/research-starters/research-starters-worldwide-deaths-world-war

Nazi Gold . (n.d.). Retrieved from wikipedia.org: https://en.wikipedia.org/wiki/Nazi_gold

News, B. (2002). *True-blue bids for Senate.* Retrieved from news.bbc.co.uk: http://news.bbc.co.uk/2/hi/americas/2297471.stm

Ninja. (2013). *History of the Jesus Piece.* Retrieved from Hypemagazine: https://hypemagazine.co.za/2013/02/08/history-of-the-jesus-piece/

NOAA. (Online). *Is there gold in the ocean?* Retrieved from Ocean-Service : https://oceanservice.noaa.gov/facts/gold.html

Nostro, L. (2013). *The 20 Dumbest Rapper Purchases.* Retrieved from complex.com: https://www.complex.com/music/2013/05/the-20-dumbest-rapper-purchases/

Nuwer, R. (2014). *Here's What Actually Happens During an Execution by Molten Gold* . Retrieved from Smithsonianmag.com: https://www.smithsonianmag.com/smart-news/heres-what-happened-people-who-were-executed-having-molten-gold-poured-down-their-throat-180951695/

Oh, M. (2005). *Bling Bling: Hip Hop's Crown Jewels* . Wenner Publishing .

Onlygold. (2019). *200 Years of Gold Prices Historical gold prices since 1792.* Retrieved from onlygold.com: http://onlygold.com/m/Prices/Prices200Years.asp

Openculture. (2014). Retrieved from Openculture.com: http://www.openculture.com/2014/01/five-hardcore-deaths-suffered-by-roman-emperors.html

Owen, J. (n.d.). *Lost Inca Gold*. Retrieved from nationalgeographic.-com: https://www.nationalgeographic.com/archaeology-and-history/archaeology/lost-inca-gold/

PBS. (2018). *The Gold Rush Impact on Native Tribes*. Retrieved from http://www.pbs.org/wgbh/americanexperience/features/goldrush-value-land/

Peterson, R. H. (1977). *The Bonanza Kings: The Social Origins and Business Behavior of Western Mining Entrepreneurs 1870–1900.* Lincoln:University of Nebraska Press.

PICKETT, M. (2017). *COLLOIDAL SILVER TURNS YOU BLUE—BUT CAN IT SAVE YOUR LIFE?* Retrieved from Wired.com: https://www.wired.com/story/does-colloidal-silver-work/

Pierre Vilar, J. W. (2011). *A History of Gold and Money 1450-1920.* Verso.

Pierre Vilar, J. W. (2011). *A History of Gold and Money 1450-1920.* Verso .

Pletcher, K. (2013). *The Age of Exploration: From Christopher Columbus to Ferdinand Magellan.* Rosen Education Service.

Powell, J. (2014). *A day-by-day account of Ottawa's history by James Powell "OPERATION "FISH".* Retrieved from TODAYINOTTAWASHISTORY.WORDPRESS.COM: https://todayinottawashistory.wordpress.com/2014/10/15/operation-fish/

Providentmetals. (2019). *Bullion vs. Numismatic Coins.* Retrieved from Providentmetals.com: https://www.providentmetals.-com/knowledge-center/precious-metals-resources/bullion-vs-numismatic-coins.html

Purestcolloids. (2019). *History gold.* Retrieved from Purestcolloids.-com: https://www.purestcolloids.com/history-gold.php

Purestcolloids. (n.d.). *History Silver* . Retrieved from Purestcolloid-s.com: https://www.purestcolloids.com/history-silver.php

Quick, A. (2007). *Deeper Roots* . DPB Printers and Booksellers .

Quintana, M. (2010). *ASHANTI EMPIRE/ ASANTE KINGDOM (18TH TO LATE 19TH CENTURY).* Retrieved from Blackpast.org: https://www.blackpast.org/global-african-history/ashanti-empire-asante-kingdom-18th-late-19th-century/

Quirkyscience. (2014). *CHARACTERISTICS OF A HIGH MASS STAR*. Retrieved from Quirkyscience.com: https://www.quirky-science.com/characteristics-high-mass-star/

Radford, B. (2017). *Leprechauns: Facts About the Irish Trickster Fairy*. Retrieved from Livescience.com: https://www.livescience.-com/37626-leprechauns.html

Reasons To Own Natural Gold. (n.d.). Retrieved from Naturalgold-trader.com.: https://www.naturalgoldtrader.com/Reasons-To-Own-Natural-Gold.html

Reggie Osse, G. T. (2006). *Bling: The Hip-Hop Jewelry Book* . Bloomsbury USA .

Reid, M. (2019). *Corrupt Maduro has broken his country. Now, democracy must have its day*. Retrieved from theguardian.com: https://www.theguardian.com/commentisfree/2019/jan/27/no-pity-for-corrupt-maduro-who-has-broken-his-country-democracy-must-have-its-day

Rensberger, B. (1976, May 24). *Solomon's Mine Believed Found*. Retrieved from New York Times: https://www.nytimes.-com/1976/05/24/archives/solomons-mine-believed-found.html

Richards, L. L. (2007). *The California Gold Rush and the coming of the Civil War*. Alfred A. Knopf.

Rickards, J. (2017). *The Truth About the Fort Knox Gold*. Retrieved from https://dailyreckoning.com/truth-fort-knox-gold/

Roberts, B. (2017). *A Brief History of Bling: Hip-Hop Jewelry*. . Retrieved from Highsnobiety.com: https://www.highsnobiety.-com/2017/04/05/hip-hop-jewelry/

RODRIGUEZ, J. (2007). *REAL 'AMERICAN GANGSTER' FRANK LUCAS TALKS ABOUT HANGING WITH DIDDY'S DAD, POSSIBLE SEQUEL*. Retrieved from MTV.com: http://www.mtv.-com/news/1573648/real-american-gangster-frank-lucas-talks-about-hanging-with-diddys-dad-possible-sequel/

Rudolph, B. (1988, August 29th). *Big Bill for a Bullion Binge*. Retrieved from TimeMagazine.com: http://content.time.-com/time/magazine/article/0,9171,968272,00.html

Schudel, M. (2014). *Nelson Bunker Hunt, Texas oil baron who lost much of his fortune, dies at 88.* Retrieved from washingtonpost.com: https://www.washingtonpost.com/business/nelson-bunker-hunt-texas-oil-baron-who-lost-much-of-his-fortune-dies-at-88/2014/10/22/81739876-5a02-11e4-8264-deed989ae9a2_story.html?noredirect=on&utm_term=.5dc2d8a88b14

Schulz, A. (2013). *GOLD IN MORE MODERN HISTORY:.* Retrieved from goldgold.com: http://www.goldgold.com/focus-on-gold.html

Script, B. B. (2001). *Baby Boy Script - Dialogue Transcript.* Retrieved from Script-o-rama.com: http://www.script-o-rama.com/movie_scripts/b/baby-boy-script-transcript.html

Scurria, A. (2019). *Venezuela Sued Over Bond Default.* Retrieved from wsj.com: https://www.wsj.com/articles/venezuela-sued-over-bond-default-11547505159?mod=searchresults&page=2&pos=19

sdbullion. (n.d.). *Silver Prices Price of Silver Today & Historical Silver Price Charts* . Retrieved from sdbullion.com: https://sdbullion.com/silver-prices

Seaman, R. M. (Ed.). (2013). *Conflict in the Early Americas: An Encyclopedia of the Spanish Empire's Aztec, Incan, and Mayan Conquests.* ABC-CLIO.

Sehgal, K. (2015). *Coined: The Rich Life of Money and How Its History Has Shaped Us.* Grand Central Publishing .

SENTINEL, S. (2017). *What is the Turnover Chain?* Retrieved from sun-sentinel.com: https://www.sun-sentinel.com/sports/miami-hurricanes/fl-sp-turnover-chain-miami-hurricanes-explainer-20171110-story.html

Serena, K. (2018). *The Story Of Bernhard Goetz — The Mugging Victim Turned New York's "Subway Vigilante".* Retrieved from allthatsinteresting.com: https://allthatsinteresting.com/bernhard-goetz

Shapiro, G. (2018). *China will surpass US to be world's largest economy — it's time for us to shift gears.* Retrieved from Foxnews.com: https://www.foxnews.com/opinion/china-will-surpass-us-to-be-worlds-largest-economy-its-time-for-us-to-shift-gears

Sheales, F. (n.d.). *The history, significance and usage of Asante royal regalia* . Retrieved from www.britishmuseum.org: https://www.britishmuseum.org/research/online_research_catalogues/ag/asante_gold_regalia/ii_gold-working/iiiii_gold-working_-continued.aspx

Sheffer, D. J. (2013). *Conflict in the Early Americas: An Encyclopedia of the Spanish Empire's Aztec, Inca, and Mayan Conquests.* . ABC-CLIO: Santa Barbara.

Sheldon, K. E. (2005). *Historical Dictionary of Women in Sub-Saharan Africa.* Scarecrow Press.

Singer, G. (2007, 1 8). *Taino Gold.* Retrieved from The Voice of the Taino People Online: http://uctp.blogspot.com/2007/01/taino-gold.html

Skousen, M. (n.d.). *The 21st Century Gold Standard: Bitcoin!* Retrieved from markskousen.com: https://www.markskousen.-com/the-21st-century-gold-standard-bitcoin/

Snapp, M. (2017). *All That Glitters: Uncovering Sardis, Ancient City of Gold.* Retrieved from Alumni.berkeley.edu: https://alumni.berkeley.e-du/california-magazine/just-in/2017-11-22/all-glitters-uncovering-sardis-ancient-city-gold

Socrates. (430 BC). *Musings.* Ahtens: Self Published.

Soniak, M. (Online). *How much gold is in a gold metal.* Retrieved from Mentalfloss: http://mentalfloss.com/article/31383/how-much-gold-gold-medal

Stylemotivation. (n.d.). *Jewelry according to your zodiac sign.* Retrieved from Stylemotivation.com: http://www.stylemotivation.-com/jewelry-according-to-your-zodiac-sign/

T.M. International. (2018). *A New Solution to Mining Rock Bursts.* Retrieved from tmi2001.com: https://www.tmi2001.com/mining-rock-burst-solutions

Taneja, R. (2018). *"Golden Baba" Is Back In Kanwar Pilgrimage, With Extra Gold.* Retrieved from https://www.ndtv.com/india-news/golden-baba-is-back-in-kanwar-yatra-with-extra-gold-1893163

Temescu, L. (2007). *20 Things You Didn't Know About... Gold.* Retrieved from http://discovermagazine.com/2007/dec/20-things-you-didn2019t-know-about-gold

The Legend of Montezumas gold. (2018, 05 06). Retrieved from globalintergold.info: https://www.globalintergold.info/en/the-legend-of-montezuma-s-gold-zo77/

Tietze, H. W. (n.d.). *Youthing How to reverse the ageing process and cure age related diseases.* Harald Tietze Publications.

Tim Gaynor, T. Z. (2011). *Gaddafi caught like "rat" in a drain, humiliated and shot.* Retrieved from Reuters.com: https://www.reuters.-com/article/us-libya-gaddafi-finalhours/gaddafi-caught-like-rat-in-a-drain-humiliated-and-shot-idUSTRE79K43S20111021

tradingeconomics. (2019). *Libya Gold Reserves.* Retrieved from tradingeconomics.com: https://tradingeconomics.com/libya/gold-reserves

value, 3. y. (n.d.). Retrieved from http://pair.offshore.ai/38yearcycle/

Vedas, L. i. (2018). *21 + Health Benefits Wearing Gold Jewelry, Says Science.* Retrieved from lifeinvedas.com: https://www.lifeinvedas.-com/21-health-benefits-wearing-gold-jewelry-says-science/

Voylla. (2016). *Which Jewelry to Wear According To Your Zodiac Sign.* Retrieved from Voylla.com: https://www.voylla.com/blog/jewelry-wear-according-zodiac-sign-scarily-accurate/

Washingtontimes. (2009). *Confounding America's ideals.* Retrieved from Washingtontimes.com: https://www.washingtontimes.-com/news/2009/aug/02/confounding-americas-ideals/

Wasson, D. L. (2017). *Valerian.* Retrieved from Ancient.eu: https://www.ancient.eu/valerian/

Weatherford, J. (1997). *The History of Money.* Crown Publishers Inc.

Week, T. (2012, October 5). *Why Did the U.S. Abandon the Gold Standard?* Retrieved from MentalFloss.com: https://www.mentalfloss.-com/article/12715/why-did-us-abandon-gold-standard

What is Monatomic Gold? (2019). Retrieved from subtle.energy: https://subtle.energy/monatomic-gold/

Wikipedia. (n.d.). Retrieved from Wikipedia.com: https://en.wikipedia.org/wiki/Kelvin_Martin

Wikipedia. (2007). *Stan Jones (Libertarian politician).* Retrieved from Wikipedia.org: https://en.wikipedia.org/wiki/Stan_Jones_(Libertarian_politician)

Wikipedia. (n.d.). *Gold Rush.* Retrieved from Wikipedia.com: https://en.wikipedia.org/wiki/Gold_rush

Woodie, B. (2011). *Hip Hop and the Crack Generation.* Retrieved from counterpunch.org: https://www.counterpunch.org/2011/09/27/hip-hop-and-the-crack-generation/

Wootton, A. (2006). *Earth's Inner Fort Knox.* Retrieved from http://discovermagazine.com/2006/sep/innerfortknox

Zhang, S. (2013). *Terrifying Facts About the World's Deepest Gold Mine.* Retrieved from gizmodo.com: https://gizmodo.com/terrifying-facts-about-the-worlds-deepest-gold-mine-1484301368

NOTES

INTRODUCTION

1. Christopher Columbus, who was unable to communicate with the Taino Indians, kidnapped several as interpreters in search of gold in the Bahamas. Columbus desire to find the source of certain amulets and nose rings worn by the Taino made from the yellow metal, which the Taino called guanin and the Spanish called oro had been obtained through trade with their Lucayan's neighbors who inhabited large islands to the south; today called Cuba and Puerto Rico. Many enslaved Taino's died after enduring the labor of mining for gold and disease brought on by European illnesses.

1. GOLD'S ORIGINS FORGED IN THE COSMOS

1. Researcher at Michigan State discovered a bacterium that can produce pure gold in 2009. The bacteria Cupriavidus metallidurans can turn gold chloride—a toxic chemical liquid you can find in nature—into 99.9% pure gold.
2. Scientist Hans Bethe in the 1930s discovered this nuclear fusion was how the Sun emitted its source of energy.
3. At the moment, there is no way to physically destroy gold. Melting it with acid or heating it to high temperatures just break's it down to liquid form, but it never evaporates or turns into a gas. It's truly immortal.

2. THE SHINING DAWN OF THE ANCIENT WORLD

1. As a sign of respect for the Sun, people of ancient times would wear gold to show reverence. Ancient man found mental, spiritual, and physical purification in gold's properties and connected to astrology in the distant past.

THE PHARAOH'S DESTINY

1. Pharaohs on special occasions would eat a type of ancient bread called emmer or farro from Egyptian harvests. This bread had monoatomic gold salt added to the yeast before baking to increase brain function for those who ate it allegedly.
2. The Shebyu collar consisted of five rows of circular gold beads strung side by side into a clasp. The collars were often formed entirely of gold. Worn by New

Kingdom Pharaohs, the collar was also rewarded for bravery or distinguished service to others outside the royal family.

SALT FOR GOLD & GOLD FOR SALT

1. Mansa Musa had so much gold the profits held to build up Timbuktu establishing it as a hub to trade gold, salt, silks, and an educational hub.

THE GOLD FIELDS OF WEST AFRICA

1. In 1921, African road workers discovered the stool and stole some of the gold ornaments. They were taken into protective custody before being tried according to local custom and sentenced to banishment.

THE LAST EMPEROR OF THE LEGENDARY KINGDOM IN THE ANDES

1. Machu Picchu, also known as "The Lost City of the Incas" was founded around 1450 and was built for Inca Emperor Pachacuti (1438-1472); the mystical estate was abandoned by the Inca in 1572.
2. After the assassination of Francisco Pizarro by a group hired by Almagro's former adherents in June 1541, Valverde fled to Panama, where his brother had been appointed as governor by Pizarro. While staying on Puná Island, in Ecuador, Valverde was captured and put to death by the local indigenous people on 31 October 1541.

MONTEZUMA'S GOLD & THE AZTEC'S BLOODY LAST STAND

1. Montezuma's vast kingdom caused hatred towards him by many other indigenous Mexican tribes he ruled over. Cortés used this vital information to find weaknesses in Montezuma's power structure and coerced enemies of the Aztecs to sack the city.
2. Jadestone was as valuable to the Aztecs as gold. Jadestone was considered to keep the wearer from harm and attract good luck. Other stones were added to silver and gold ornaments, such as amethyst, opal, and turquoise.
3. Montezuma was heavily guarded and quarantined from the public. According to Buddy Levy, Cortés's behavior to touch the King created tension Montezuma should have picked up on.
4. According to a legend, while staying in one of Montezuma's palaces, the Spaniards knocked down a brick wall and discovered a large room full of precious riches. There were piles of gold jewelry, gems, as well as expensive fabrics. The treasures belonged to former Aztec emperor Axayacatl, the predecessor of Montezuma.

5. This slaughter of Aztec citizens by the hands of Alvarado took place during the Feast of Toxcatl, which was a sacred day for the Aztec's dedicated to the God Tezcatlipoca.

NATIVE AMERICAN SLAVE LABOR & ITS ROLE IN THE GOLD RUSH

1. Dr. Claud Anderson explains the gold rush, Native American slave owners, and the lack of involvement in obtaining the wealth gold provided in his book *"Black Labor White Wealth."*
2. Mount Rushmore was originally called The Six Grandfathers, a section of the sacred Black Hills of the Lakota Tribe. Gold was discovered in the area around 1877, and the U.S. Government seized the land coupled with bounty hunters who earned $300 for each Native killed, decimating the Lakota Tribe.

THE WORLD'S DEEPEST GOLD MINE

1. Mining is a dangerous job. The deeper mines go into the Earth in search of gold, the riskier they become.

5. THE ESOTERIC VALUE OF GOLD & SILVER'S MYSTERIOUS HEALING POWER

1. Unknown property in gold assists in healing the nervous and endocrine system. Research is still conducted to identify the specific ingredients that provide the potential healing gold provides

GOLD: METAPHYSICAL PROPERTIES & POWERS

1. People with Jupiter in the 11th house should always wear gold, whether it be a ring or chain. This is an example of Jupiter placement and if gold will benefit you while wearing it.

GRAMS & GOLD CHAINS

1. Excerpt from Bling The Hip-Hop Jewelry Book by Reggie Ossé

FUN FACT

1. In 2005, Eric B. & Rakim released their third compilation album entitled "Gold" which contains remixes and extended versions of their classic records.

HOW FORT KNOX GOT ITS GOLD & WHY ITS KEPT THERE

1. Before Fort Knox being built, the Treaty of Fort Laramie was enacted in 1851. Under this treaty and other past scenarios, Native Americans lost their lands and gold mineral wealth surrounding the Kentucky area to settlers. This treaty additionally allowed the government to construct railroad tracks and build forts to quell the perceived fear of the Native American tribe's hostility towards settlers.

THE HUNT BROTHERS

1. The Hunt Brothers lost many assets in their attempt to corner the silver market, including their stake in Placid Oil, as collateral for the loan they obtained. However, the value of their assets (mainly holdings in oil, sugar, and real estate) declined steadily during the 1980s, and their estimated net wealth fell from $5 billion in 1980 to less than $1 billion in 1988. (Rudolph, 1988)

ABOUT THE AUTHOR

Dawdu M. Amantanah, a best-selling author of several books Death of a Rose: Rise of the Black Petunia, Cover Me In Gold: The History, Horrors & Other Unknown Facts About Gold, and the forthcoming The Bit on Digital Coins: A quick practical guide to understanding cryptocurrency. An alumnus of Southern New Hampshire University School of Business before discovering a passion for writing, Dawdu worked for technology and financial institutions such as J.P. Morgan Chase and State Street Bank.

Made in the USA
Las Vegas, NV
03 November 2026

57423304R00159